CULTURE
IS AN
INSIDE
JOB

SCOTT McGOHAN

CULTURE IS AN INSIDE JOB

EMBRACING SELF-AWARENESS TO INSPIRE AN AUTHENTIC ORGANIZATION

HAWTHORNE HEIGHTS
PUBLISHING

Published by Hawthorne Heights Publishing, Springboro
www.scottmcgohan.com

Edited and designed by Girl Friday Productions
www.girlfridayproductions.com

Cover design: David Fassett
Project management: Mari Kesselring

Image credits: cover © Rawpixel/Wit

ISBN (paperback): 979-8-9876923-0-1
ISBN (ebook): 979-8-9876923-1-8

Library of Congress Control Number: 2023908584

CONTENTS

Preface ix
Introduction xiii

PART I: HOW WE GOT HERE

Chapter 1 | The Death of a Destructive Hero 3

    Hello, My Name Is Scott, and I'm a Destructive Hero—Case Study . . *4*

    Are You a (Destructive) Hero? *6*

    Add It Up: The Cost of a Destructive Hero *7*

    Drop the Mask *8*

    "A Soft Pillow" *9*

    Your People—Only a Means to Your End? *11*

    Reflection: Let's Go Inside *12*

Chapter 2 | An Authentic Employee Experience 14

    Relationship Is the Currency of Culture *16*

    What Do You Love? *19*

    Destructive Hero Rehab *21*

    Do Unto Employees as You Would Have Them Do Unto You *24*

    Reflection: Let's Go Inside *26*

Chapter 3 | The Culture Gap 28

    Culture ≠ Reputation *29*

    What Exactly Is Character? *32*

    More than Ping-Pong Tables *33*

    You Might Be Lying to Yourself *35*

    Voice Mails, Golf, and Telling the Truth *36*

    Everyone Has a Culture (and a Culture Gap) *40*

Reflection: Let's Go Inside *41*

Chapter 4 | Culture Blind Spots 42

What's It Like to Work for Your Company? *43*

The Four Cultural Behaviors *45*

What Do You See in Your Blind Spot? *47*

Truth Tellers and Grudges *49*

A Culture in Trouble *52*

What You Tolerate, You Encourage *53*

Reflection: Let's Go Inside *56*

PART II: FOUNDATIONAL PRINCIPLES

Chapter 5 | A Culture Committed to Change 61

Closing the Gap *63*

The Five Senses of Your Culture *65*

Making Your Culture Look Right *66*

Making Your Culture Feel Right *70*

Making Your Culture Sound Right *75*

Making Your Culture Taste Right *77*

Making Your Culture Smell Right *78*

Reflection: Let's Go Inside (If you do only one exercise

in this book, please do this one.) *79*

Chapter 6 | Culture with a Cause 81

What Smells in Here? *81*

A Motive for Giving Back *83*

Stumping for a Cause *85*

Reflection: Let's Go Inside *87*

Chapter 7 | Culture Heroes 89

Catch the Culture Bug *90*

The Four Cs *91*

Calling on Your Heroes *95*

Don't Let Your Culture Become a Crime Scene 97

Reflection: Let's Go Inside 98

Chapter 8 | A Culture of Cooperation 100

Customer Culture Journey Mapping 102

A Spiderweb Is Full of Straight Lines 105

"Quit Doing My Job!" 107

Singing the Unsung. 108

Can You See the Problem and Ignore the Noise? 109

Reflection: Let's Go Inside 111

PART III: BUILDING FOR THE FUTURE

Chapter 9 | A Workforce-Attracting Culture 115

The Most Important Word 116

Attracting (and Keeping) Top Performers 118

The Third Most Important Word: Thanks. 119

Try to Be Specific 120

A Helping Hand from the Top 122

Reflection: Let's Go Inside 123

Chapter 10 | A Culture for Everyone 125

Filling Your Building with Good, Smart (Diverse) People 127

Don't Pick on Generations; You Are a Part of One 129

Who's Comfortable? 132

Reflection: Let's Go Inside 133

Chapter 11 | A Culture of Stop, Keep, and Start 134

Why I Hate Glassdoor Reviews . . . and Absolutely Love Them. 136

Feed It Forward 138

Just Because You Hear Doesn't Mean You're Listening 139

Lean Into Listening 140

360 Degrees of You 143

Reflection: Let's Go Inside 146

Chapter 12 | The Future-Proof Culture 147
  EI, AI, and How to Save Your Employees' Jobs *148*
  The Future Is Inside of You *149*
  The Mirror Is a Wonderful Place to Find a Friend *152*
  Not Just a Tool, but a Way of Life 154
  Life Has Terms; Learn How to Embrace Them *155*
  Tell Stories to Technology-Proof Your Workforce *158*
  Reflection: Let's Go Inside *160*

Conclusion | The Mirror Is a Wonderful
    Place to Find a Friend 162

Bonus | Culture Through the Lens of a Crisis 168
  An Organization Has a Heartbeat *169*
  Focus Matters *172*
  Living the MB Culture *174*
  A New, Exciting Chapter for MB *182*
  Reflection: Let's Go Inside *185*

Acknowledgments 187
Appendix: Sample Employee Survey 189
Notes 195
About the Author 197

PREFACE

I grew up in a wonderful family. I lived in a loving home. I attended terrific schools. A picture-perfect life by anyone's standards. All that should have been enough for me. But I wanted more, a *lot* more. For decades, I wasn't sure where the desire for more came from.

Maybe having a twin brother had something to do with it. As a child, I struggled to find my own identity. *Who am I without my brother?* I tried to be different for the sake of being different. One noticeable difference was the gift of my lazy eye, which only made matters worse. It made people look at me differently—the *wrong* kind of differently. Or so I thought. I was also dyslexic, which made learning and reading difficult. I didn't like myself, and I thought others didn't like me, either. Today, I know this was my perception—but back then, it felt like the truth.

During my sophomore year of high school, in the back seat of a Chevette on the way to a Cincinnati Reds game, I met a friend who made me feel bigger, stronger, and more courageous. That little friend was alcohol. My new personality was born. For the first time, I was funny. People laughed *with* me instead of *at* me. I thought I was more popular and friendlier. At least, that was my perception. I learned the hard way that alcohol wasn't a friend, and it certainly wasn't the answer—I flunked out of college and got a job at a jewelry store. There, I met my future wife. As soon as I saw her, I knew we would just be friends. She was too pretty, too nice, and too smart for a guy like me. We did become friends, but that friendship turned into the best relationship I have ever had. She saw something in me I couldn't see. And for that, I will always be grateful.

Fast-paced work then became my drug of choice. The rat race was my quest. If I couldn't *find* my self-worth, I could at least *buy* it. Cars, houses, clothes, electronics—you name it. If I couldn't stand myself on the inside, maybe my outside could mask the pain. I thought performance plus the opinions of others equaled self-worth. And let me tell you, that is terrible math to live by.

A Destructive Hero was born.

The fast pace I kept turned out to be both a curse and a blessing. By the grace of God and the love of the people closest to me, I found my self-worth. It took truth, honesty, and lessons on the meaning of life. It rarely had anything to do with material items. You see, my family and friends loved me when I had no capacity to love myself. And in turn, that unselfish love taught me how to love myself and others.

I hope my journey will be useful to you. I know I'm not alone in my struggles, and if you can learn from my mistakes, I've fulfilled my purpose. Someone told me long ago that your brain is like a bad neighborhood—you shouldn't be there alone. I wasn't alone. I was with a loving God, loving people, and a surrendering heart that allowed me to watch the death of my Destructive Hero. That death led me to rebuild myself from the inside out versus the outside in.

My journey began by exploring when I was most comfortable with who I was. When I was younger, I enjoyed writing poetry, but society (or in some cases, I) told lies to myself that boys shouldn't write poetry. I enjoyed drawing, but I saw others with much more talent and decided I did not have the talent to continue. I enjoyed being alone in a creative spirit that would carry me to faraway places, creating inventions that could change my world.

At some point, I just stopped growing up. I wasn't happy with who I was, so I conformed to what I thought others wanted from me instead of what made me happy. Such a sad and warped sense of self.

The work included going back, in my mind, to the woods behind our house, my treehouse, and deeper into my childhood to attempt to define what had happened and why. What I discovered was not as dramatic as I had expected. You see, I thought it would be an event or a certain person, place, or thing that had stolen my ability to find peace.

I was hoping it would be as simple as that. Instead, I was forced to look at my journey over time and the slow burn of my perception versus reality. My reality shifted into a new understanding about my defects of character and where they came alive in my life. This work began to take shape and provide the power of clarity when I explored the resentments I had against people, places, and things.

The truth began to come alive, and a beacon of hope ignited that today didn't have to be the same as yesterday, and tomorrow didn't have to be the same as today.

Everyone and everything can be beautifully redeemed inside of acceptance. When I accepted my past, with all of the bruises and scars it provided, a bright headlight revealed a beautiful new road to restoration.

Thank you to all who taught me. Thank you to all who loved me anyway, both then and today. Learning to love myself allowed me to love others in ways more amazing than I thought I was capable of. So please, come take a ride with me. Together, we can create amazing experiences for ourselves and others.

INTRODUCTION

Every organization has a culture because every organization has people. Products are innovated by people, manufactured by people, packaged by people, shipped by people, bought by people, and thrown away by people. Like businesses and the products they sell, culture is about people. Always has been and, by the grace of God, always will be.

I came to believe this: "What we think is what we believe, what we believe is what we give to the world, and what we give to the world is what the world sees in us." In other words, what you think your organization is, is what your people will believe to be true about your company—or, deeper than that, what they believe about you as the leader. If that is their belief system, then that is what they will give back to your organization and what your customers will see.

This can get fairly complicated, but it is important that you as the leader and your leadership team behave as you want your organization to believe. For example, if a sense of urgency is a critical element internally and externally, but you and others do not reply to emails or call people back, then those are just words—and actions trump words every time.

Creating an organizational culture is critical and, in my opinion, one of the most important ingredients to inspire your people, customers, and the communities you serve.

Here is where we get sideways with this conversation, or the passion to create an "inspiring culture." Like me, many want what they don't have, and they can't get what they haven't earned. In other words, a mission, vision, or value might *sound* good—maybe even quite compelling—but it is worse than something fake if it is not deeply rooted in ourselves. It becomes an organizational lie.

I thought I had a great handle on culture until a few years ago when I met a business coach named Anne Thompson. She runs an organization named Integrity First Coaching. She was patient and spent time understanding me, our business, and our desired state.

I wanted to get right to work, and like most great coaches, she listened more than she spoke and did her best to create a template to make the work come alive inside of me instead of forcing the work through my experience and competence.

She carried me through—not around, over, or under—but *through* a new journey to bring a beautiful culture alive. I gained a new vision for a vibrant future for myself and our business. I could tell our story from a heart foundation, but I had a difficult time including a business strategy. Anne provided this guidance for me and our organization.

A positive culture does three things for an organization:

1. Helps meet the organization's vision and mission
2. Allows the organization to adapt to change
3. Empowers people to thrive

When these are understood and respected individually and together, it is much easier to accomplish them from an organizational standpoint. I am confident it doesn't matter whether you sell hot dogs, lemonade, or technology; meeting these three objectives can and will make your business stronger, better, and more vibrant. Here's the secret question: Where are you in these three areas of your life: what you stand for, what you care about, and what you leave space for? If you don't know the answer to that question, then you limit your ability to adapt to change and your capacity to thrive.

If you are asking your workforce to inspire customers or communities to make a difference, but you are not inspiring and may even be a tyrant, then that's an organizational lie. If you are asking to keep up with technology and innovation but are too stubborn to invest, that's an organizational lie. If you want your workforce to thrive by growing their income, sending kids off to college, buying homes, and giving back, but your compensation model is stingy, that's an organizational lie.

Whether you call it a lie, a stretch, a marketing strategy, or an out-of-state consultant's advice, as leaders, we must start with our internal culture. Your vision (the desired state of where you want your organization to be, an almost unattainable, faraway place of wonder, beauty, and transformation) and mission (the "how" you will get there) come first. Good questions to ask yourself are:

1. What is your mission and vision?
2. What is your ability and energy to change?
3. Do you inspire yourself, your family, and your people to thrive?

It's up to the people *around* you, your family, friends, suppliers, customers, and employees, to say whether it's a good culture, a bad culture, or in between. You don't dictate the culture, nor does the CEO, the president, management, the words painted on the walls, a brochure, a website, or the person at the front desk.

Have you ever asked your people what they think of your organization's culture? Is your company a great place to work, where everyone feels like their work matters and, more importantly, like *they* matter? Or do they feel like their worth depends on putting their heads down, meeting deadlines, and keeping the company profitable?

Go even further and ask them about you. Culture is an inside job—go inside and find out. We learn so much when we go inside of ourselves and our organization to gain greater understanding.

Think about buying your first house. You probably drove around and looked at houses, sometimes catching yourself in neighborhoods you could not afford but dreamt of one day living in. The outside of the homes looked pristine; many do. But when you went inside, you began to see the faults, cracks, and undesirable aspects you didn't like and you wanted to change.

The day your employees start work, they have a vision of what they will see, hear, and feel inside of the organization. If a disconnect exists, it's hard to try to inspire a workforce.

Now, I want to ask you a different question. Have you ever asked your people what they think or, more importantly, how they feel about your organization's culture and heard an honest answer?

Someone once said, "Life is a wonderful teacher, and she rarely gets an apple on her desk." Well, I have taken a lot of bites out of apples, not because I like apples but because I once was more arrogant, stubborn, and egotistical, which was a result of being a scared and fearful little boy who never really grew up.

How did this happen?

Every hero has sidekicks. Alas, all too often, heroes treat those sidekicks like they're replaceable. I've done it, and I've seen it several times throughout my thirty-year career. A high-achieving leader, who we will call an *individual contributor*, gets a big ego, and that ego leaves a path of destruction all the way to human resources and back.

In my experience, *these* leaders or *individual contributors* are tempted to wear the cape of the **Destructive Hero**. They have big ideas and get even bigger results. They're larger-than-life legends with a reputation that everyone in their field envies. In person, these heroes are charming and witty. On paper, they're top performers who everyone wants to emulate.

On paper.

In reality, their selfish actions don't paint such a nice picture. Destructive Heroes are *me first, everyone else second.* They're usually:

- Perceived as successful
- Responsible for large accounts
- A top, if not the very best, salesperson
- A relative of an owner, founder, or C-suite member
- A person you frequently bring up in conversation
- A person who gets **you or your organization** "drunk" on their results (they dazzle you with their achievements)

I should know. I was one. I am not proud of this part of my life, but today, I don't hide or use my past to beat myself up. I try to use this part of my life to be useful to others.

Each chapter that follows includes a series of reflection questions at the end. I encourage you to simply think about them. *Surrender* is an incredible word, and its roots consist of another word, *agreement.* You see, to surrender, we need to submit to conditions under an agreement. I didn't ask for many of the situations I went through. Looking back, I did the best I could do. Today, I am so blessed to have walked through my new agreement of understanding my past, today, and what tomorrow could bring.

I had built a life from the outside in instead of the inside out. My surrender included going back inside and doing deep inner work regarding who I wanted to be and who I was called to be versus what society told me I should be. That was a lie; today, the truth is clearer, and so is my life.

Are you ready to join me? Let's go inside.

PART I

How We Got Here

CHAPTER 1

The Death of a Destructive Hero

Seventeen years ago, my assistant, Victoria, came into my office. She closed the door but didn't sit down. She always sits down.

"Scott, you have values painted on your wall, like 'family' and 'integrity,'" she said. "But you don't exhibit a single one of them. I have my own values, and you torque every single one of them every day. Today is my last day."

Mic drop. I was stunned. She'd been my right hand ever since I'd first started at my dad's company. She'd always seemed happy. Content, at the very least. So I thought, *What does she want? Flowers? A bonus? A corner office? Whatever it takes to make sure no one else knows about this conversation . . .*

"I torque your values?" I asked. "What does that even mean?"

"You tell people you're going to call them back, and you don't. You say you're going to show up at a meeting, and you don't. You work seven days a week, and your workload and procrastination affect me and others around me."

"Oh."

No big deal. A bonus should do it. If not, I'll just tell everyone she didn't like it here . . .

"Since I'm quitting anyway, I just wanted to tell you how I felt," she said, turning to leave.

"Wait a second. Sit down, please. Don't do anything yet," I begged. "Let me ask you—what if I could break down . . . whatever this is? Would you be willing to listen, and maybe we can sort things out?"

She sighed. "Would *I* be willing to listen?"

"Yes. Let's talk about it. I will fix it. First thing tomorrow morning?"

She broke eye contact and nodded. "I'll think about it."

I followed her out of our office, trying to make small talk so people saw us together. I did it to prop up my image. I was terrified on the inside and an egotistical jerk on the outside. People would ask questions for sure. The assistant to the number one sales guy in the company doesn't just quit unless something *big* happens.

"I think she's wrong," I would tell my coworkers . . . and my dad. "It's not my fault."

I believed no one saw her leave any differently than she had for years.

HELLO, MY NAME IS SCOTT, AND I'M A DESTRUCTIVE HERO—CASE STUDY

For the rest of the afternoon, I kept my office door open. No need to support any rumors I was in there stewing in my own uncertainty. No one said anything about Victoria's early departure, and I didn't bring it up.

What are people going to think about me if she leaves? I thought on the drive home. That's the thought of a self-absorbed person. Damage control mattered more than anything. I was the company's eighth overall employee. I was the founder's kid, who outproduced most by a long shot and had dominated sales for the past ten years. No one ever challenged me. My opinion on any topic was gold. After all, I was the heir to the business of a man with a sympathetic heart. I was a faithful husband and loyal father. I drove the right car, lived in the right house, wore the right clothes, and belonged to the right country club.

Success.

On paper, at least. No one had ever told me to work on *me*—who I was inside, who I *could* be, or what core values I held. So, I hadn't bothered. Until Victoria.

The next morning, she walked into my office at 7:59. I shut the door to make sure no one could hear our conversation. I spoke softly and quietly and tried to put on the mask of humility. It didn't fit; it never had.

"I want to thank you for your feedback," I said, careful not to grovel or beg. Now today, I know that facing this issue straight up would have led to a much better conversation and a shorter journey, but I had no tools to do so at the time. I continued, "I think there's another way for us to work this out other than you leaving. Can we . . . work on this? Together?"

"Maybe."

"OK. What would that look like? Maybe if I hired an executive coach to work with, and you could talk to them every day? I could also sign up for leadership classes at the University of Dayton. Would you give me a chance to change?"

She looked up to consider my offer. Deep down, she wanted out, but maybe from the goodness of her heart, she would give me a chance. "Yes. Under one condition," she said. "Every day, you and I have to meet in my workspace, and you have to ask me three questions."

"OK, sure." *Promising.* "What are the questions?"

"'Are you OK? Am I OK? Are we OK?'"

"I can do that."

"Every day for the next twelve months?"

"Yes." I gulped. "Deal."

And I thought *I* was in charge. We shook hands.

"I'll try to clean up my mess. I'll go to those meetings. And I'll call people back. From now on, I'll do what I say I'm going to do. I'll think about you more and me less."

Victoria walked out of my office with a smile on her face. I sat down at my desk to the biggest piece of humble pie I had ever eaten in my life. I was a Destructive Hero, and Victoria was the only person at my company brave enough to tell me.

ARE YOU A (DESTRUCTIVE) HERO?

Most leaders don't have a Victoria. They have people who feel the way she felt, who experience what she experienced. But they're too afraid to say anything. They could reveal their presence through anonymous company surveys, "borrowed" office supplies, and two-week notices. But they don't speak up before it's too late. To your face, they'll tell you they love working at your organization. They love the work, the perks, and the people. They love the culture. *They lie.* Because it's not the company they're leaving, it's the person they report to.

Your organization "feels like family," your people tell you. Is it a terrible, dysfunctional family with authoritarian parents whose egos keep the kids walking on eggshells all day? Or a family that enjoys spending time together, supports each other, and loves each other?

You have an idea of what people think of you and your organization. Don't rest on your truth or the hype you're reading. Be *very* careful about believing your own press. Let me say this again because many people need to hear this: **Be very careful not to believe your own press**.

It shouldn't be this way. Since you're still reading, I know *you* don't want it to be this way, either. The simplest way to measure your personal culture is to evaluate your opinion of yourself. In other words, if you don't hold yourself to a higher standard, how can you expect others to do the same?

To save my relationship with Victoria, and my dignity, *I* had to commit first. The Destructive Hero had to die so the company—and the employees—could live.

If you think a Destructive Hero is costing you and your organization, you're probably right. Chances are high they're drunk on the revenue, the client relationships, or their own ego. Or even worse, maybe *you're* the Destructive Hero. Does it matter? You bet it does. Let's calculate the financial impact a Destructive Hero has on a company.

ADD IT UP: THE COST OF A DESTRUCTIVE HERO

1. _____ Number of people dealing with a Destructive Hero
2. _____ Total annual salaries of these people
3. _____ Total salaries divided by 2,040 hours (number of work hours in a year)
4. _____ Multiply by the average number of hours each person spent dealing with the Destructive Hero this year
5. _____ Add salaries of the people who have left their positions because of this person
6. _____ Total cost of a Destructive Hero

Keep in mind that this number is only a portion of the real cost of the Destructive Hero inside your organization. It's impossible to calculate the opportunities you don't even know you've missed. If you're the Destructive Hero, it's time to come clean. You can't afford not to. To hunt other potential

Destructive Heroes in your organization (when it's really you) would be like demanding everyone show up on time to meetings when you're always late. The last thing your organization needs is for everyone else to wake up while you stay asleep. After all, leadership is an inside job. So, if you're ready to work, I'm ready to tell you my story.

DROP THE MASK

The shock of Victoria's announcement woke me up to my mistakes, my Destructive Heroism. I promised her I would hire a coach. And I promised myself that I would never put on the cape and mask of a Destructive Hero again. I was scared to death of what people would think of me if Victoria left, and I realized that left little to no room in my priorities for her—an honest thought, and the beginning of my honesty journey. I knew then that I wasn't a bad person, just a person who needed help. I'd gotten myself into the Destructive Hero uniform, and it was obvious I wasn't qualified to take it off.

I would like to say I wanted this for her and others, but deep down, I just wanted to get out of trouble, like a small child who cleans their room after making a big mistake.

A few nights after Victoria told me to ask her those three terrifying questions—"Are you OK? Am I OK? Are we OK?"—I drove my wife and our teenage children home from a company event. While they slept in the car, I wondered what *their* answers would be. Would they be too afraid to answer honestly?

I felt fear in that question, and for the first time, shame showed up. Victoria had choices, and she had defined those for me. If I didn't change, she was leaving. She was and is very competent, and she could and would have moved on. My family, on the other hand, was more complicated, and I began to believe they tolerated much worse from me. Would they, could they, tell me the truth?

When we got home, I sat down in my study and searched for the truth, spilling my thoughts one at a time. When I was younger, I used to write poetry, but society told me that boys didn't or shouldn't write poetry, so I stopped. I stopped drawing, painting, and writing. If I was on a quest for the truth, or *a* truth, maybe writing could help me. Maybe, just maybe, the truth would set me free. In my search for it, I wrote this poem:

"A SOFT PILLOW"

I lay here alone with my prizes held high,
And think of the past with a tear in my eye.
My life has been grand from the outside,
    you see,
Why is the past so dark to me?
I gathered so much more than I could
    hold,
What I now realize is that my soul has
    been sold.
You see, I lay here myself, all alone.
It hurts so badly, my heart and soul moan.
What I can't do for you is to give you your
    past.
Unfortunately, in life, time does not last.
Oh, I pray to go back; please, one more
    chance!
To see your small face and your smile
    while you dance.
Why was I so blind when you asked me to
    play?

And I looked at you and said, "Maybe
    another day."
I stood there in the flesh, but my heart
    was astray,
If I could go back, I'd give it all away.
My gift from above was you by my side,
What a fool I was to push you aside.
You're older now with children of your
    own,
I pray every day that you don't leave their
    hearts alone.
Take time to hold them and share their
    dreams.
Their little hearts aren't as small as they
    may seem.
My pillow is hard, like my heart was then.
Please, listen to me, for what I did is a sin.
You don't have much time to ask God for
    grace,
Don't do what I did and think life is a race.
Give your heart to God and tie it with a
    bow,
And someday your head will rest on a soft
    pillow.

My commitment to reform my attitude toward everyone in my life sent me back to college, to leadership programs, and to management coaching, where I would learn (and apply) how to lead beyond my own belly button, how to build an empowering culture, and how to create an outrageously positive employee experience.

It's time to rebuild my life. I started cleaning out everything I could see. I came to realize my old belief that if things looked clean and organized on the outside, people would think I had it all figured out on the inside. Another lie.

If you look in the trunk of someone's car, you get a glimpse into what their lives are like. If you'd looked in my trunk, you would have known that my life was a mess. My garage was a mess. My desk, my closet, my drawers. From the outside, things looked great, just like my life. I wanted everyone to think I had it all figured out. But open any drawer, and you would see the chaos.

My spring-cleaning frenzy drove my wife nuts. I brought garbage cans in the house. I'm not talking about small ones—I mean the giant ones with wheels. I spent weeks cleaning every aspect of my life.

It was hard work, but it felt great. I was finally organized. The big problem was that my hands were so busy cleaning, I didn't have a chance to think. When the cleaning was done, I was left wondering what to do next. Looking back, cleaning and organizing just made the problems go away for a moment. The guilt and shame kept my ego from getting too much out of control. When my hands had nothing to do, I was left with thinking, and that is when the hard work began.

I took a look at myself in the mirror. I was ready to be a kinder person, ready to be a husband who could love without expectations, ready to be a father who had time to talk and play, and ready to be a leader who could begin a journey of truth. Cleaning the physical garbage out of my life allowed me to work on the deeper garbage inside of my soul.

YOUR PEOPLE—ONLY A MEANS TO YOUR END?

I wish every leader had a Victoria. After *Forbes* proclaimed 2018 as "the year of employee experience," I knew something was off when I read Corporate America's justification for treating people better: "Employees' commitment to your company and their roles . . . is the end goal while [employee experience] is the means to that end."[1]

Wait a second! What about the *company's* commitment to their people? We're defining employee experience completely wrong. **A great culture is for the people who work *in* that culture; a great employee experience is for the** *employees*! When you treat your employees the way you want your customers treated, without a self-serving agenda, life gets clearer, simpler, and a whole lot more fun.

In the pages ahead, I'll show you how to reform your culture from the inside out (starting with you), create an authentic employee experience, and design a high-performance organization where kind, good, smart people want to work. More importantly, a place where you can begin to look in the mirror and smile at the person looking back.

You *can* change the status quo. But you'll have to look beyond the bottom line—and your own belly button—to see it. Look at your people. Because that's what they are . . . *people*. They will give their blood, sweat, and tears for your company— and for you—if they're inspired to. Will you do the same for them?

Reflection: Let's Go Inside

Self-awareness is powerful. When we turn our thoughts into words by simply putting them on paper, they can do amazing work inside of our lives. We must find the courage to move through a process. If you're like me, it took time to mess things up. Duct tape, superglue, or bubble gum will not fix these problems. They will take time, so give yourself the time you need to repair them beautifully.

1. What is your culture today?
2. What is your mission and vision?
3. What is your ability and energy to change?
4. Do you inspire yourself, your family, and your people to thrive?
5. Do you have any Destructive Hero traits today? Do you know? What are they as you know them today?
6. Do you have the tools or the relationships to repair them?
7. Do you have a truth teller in your life? If not, can you find one? If so, have you thanked them?
8. Have you considered the cost of a Destructive Hero inside of your organization? (see page 7)
9. Can you address this issue today? Why is this important to you? Why not?
10. Will you begin to address this issue? Why? Why not?

CHAPTER 2

An Authentic Employee Experience

My true teacher—my father, Pat McGohan—was so close to me, yet I was too ignorant to understand his lessons. I walked around in life with arrogant-colored glasses.

My father grew up in a two-bedroom house with a dirt-floor basement. He drove a milk truck when he was fourteen and earned a full-ride golf scholarship. My mother had my twin brother and me when my father was a sophomore in college. He believed life shouldn't be all about how much you can sell or how much you can make. It's about *who* you are while you're doing it. Even when the going got tough, he was the same person at work, at home, and on the golf course.

I should've learned this lesson from my dad the first time around. As a young up-and-comer at McGohan Brabender, I watched him turn the Island of Misfit Toys into a culture so high performing we buried all of our competitors. But *how* he did it made no sense.

"You're doing a great job. I'm very proud of you," he said to an employee who'd made a big mistake. A fireable offense, according to the books I read.

"Everybody needs encouragement, and the people who deserve it the least need it most," Dad told me privately once the person's spirits lifted. "Let me say that again. *The people who deserve it the least need it most.*" It took me over a decade of hearing this before I got it.

That's not how you do culture, I thought. *Coddling is not culture. Dad's sappy. Maybe unrealistic!*

During business hours, my dad wandered into employees' workspaces and looked around their desks. Whatever personal effects he saw, he asked them about: "Is that a picture of you and your children on vacation? Where did you go? I didn't know you liked golf. Where's your favorite place to play?"

He never rerouted small talk into work topics. Ever. Was that a waste of time? Not to him. I can't count the number of adult's and children's golf clubs, toys, and other items he carried into the office to give to people. Maybe they needed those things, maybe not. But that was his way of showing them he believed in them. Years later, I'm grateful for his example.

"Summer's almost here, so school's almost out," he once said to a working mother in human resources. "Do you have a sitter lined up? Until you do, let me know, and we'll put some toys in that spare office."

One day, all hell broke loose during a shareholder meeting—hijacked by a heated discussion over a new hire. But my dad walked out of that office like the sun was shining.

"Be careful what you let people see," he told me. "You represent the organization. If you're angry, the company is angry. Nobody wants to work for an angry company. Remember, folks are watching you."

"What does that have to do with selling group insurance to the biggest employers in Dayton?" I asked, reminding him what our business was supposed to do.

"Everything. We care about our people first and how they

can benefit us second," he said, smiling the way only a father does. "We treat our employees the way we want our customers treated. If I'm going to ask someone to do something for me, whether it's an employee or a customer, I need to have a relationship with them first."

I wish I'd known then that the guy was on to something. My dad was an expert in a different kind of culture: a culture of love. His love for people—*his* people—was a tool he used to build one of the largest independent health insurance brokers in the United States. He wasn't a perfect man, and that's OK. Nobody can stand people who think they're perfect.

People like me. I was so busy driving for perfection and judging others that I was blind to my character defects and the impact those defects had on others.

RELATIONSHIP IS THE CURRENCY OF CULTURE

My wife deserves a medal for loving me when I was a Destructive Hero. She must have seen something in me that I couldn't comprehend. Maybe she didn't know how to tell me I was a Destructive Hero, or she knew I had to figure it out on my own. Most Destructive Heroes aren't fortunate to have a relationship like ours. At times, my love was authentic and honest, but for the most part, I was trying to impress upon everyone (even my family) that I was important.

By the grace of God, my wife was much more mature, patient, and loving than I was. When I defeated the Destructive Hero within, the ring she kept on her finger was reward enough. As a reformed Destructive Hero, I don't look back on those days to torture myself. That time in my life was my teacher and may be useful to others.

At our core, many Destructive Heroes don't want to be the way they are. The problem is few people have the courage to tell us we're destructive. Society has let us behave this way for so long, we become blind to our destructiveness. I believe this behavior started as a defense mechanism to stop us from looking at ourselves too honestly. Our behavior is an escape, albeit a lonely one. Somewhere along the way, we had experiences and heard (or imagined) words that damaged our identity, our sense of self. So, we isolated ourselves, protecting us from essential human connection.

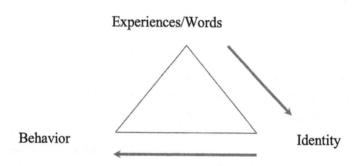

I heard a wonderful speaker named Nancy Beach walk through this process a few years ago. She spoke about how, as leaders, our roles come with obligations. Obligations, paired with a messed-up sense of identity, lead to resentment. Resentment of people, places, or things can lead to entitlement. And entitlement, when we expect something but don't get it, leads us to search for an escape.

We can escape through alcohol, food, drugs, sex, gambling, and gossiping, to name a few. We pick one, two, or more. It's no surprise Destructive Heroes tend to have dysfunctional relationships—we don't have a good one with ourselves.

As a young man, I was arrogant—I wanted to be important, better than everyone around me. Instead of forming meaningful relationships, I bought expensive clothes, cars, and other things I didn't need. To afford them, I had to perform at a cost my family paid. When that didn't work, alcohol numbed the pain. But blame was my sharpest weapon of choice. It was never *my* fault I wasn't happy. I was working harder than anyone. It was *their* fault. I made sure everyone around me felt my resentment.

If you know a Destructive Hero, listen to them. Watch their actions. Their behavior is a force field to protect themselves. For example, many Destructive Heroes have learned they can distract and detach themselves by getting pissed off and yelling or by engaging in an equally destructive behavior—falling silent. Most people don't have the insight or courage to deal with an adult's tantrum, so they let it be. Anger and silence work, protecting them from any hurtful relationship. But that anger or silence isn't over a person or an event—it's about themselves and their self-imposed isolation.

Today, I know relationships are the most important part of our lives. The same is true for your business. Relationships—they're the currency of culture. Authentic, positive, meaningful relationships. When Victoria called me on my crap, I realized I was dead broke. All the popular business books I bought in my twenties told me to "cut the bottom 10 percent off," "squeeze people till they're empty," and "kill the weak to make room for the strong." These leaders and authors were successful; were they right?

WHAT DO YOU LOVE?

My father met a great guy named Pete Kunk, a personal coach with a company named Built to Lead in Columbus, Ohio. He is a truth teller, a great teacher, and most of all, a very patient man, even with the worst offenders (like me). My father hired him and let me believe I made the decision. Nice gesture, Dad.

When Pete helped me patch things up with Victoria, he asked me what my core values were. I gave an answer that would've made my dad cringe.

"I value sales goals and meeting them every month. I value growth. I value the company's performance plan. I value my family. Does that make sense?"

"No, it doesn't," Pete said. "What about love? Do you love your kids? Your wife?"

"Of course. But hey, my wife and I have dreams. Big house, country club, friends, and a garage full of stuff. I bought each of my kids a brand-new car on their sixteenth birthday. Why would my family think I'm not the dad and the husband I need to be?"

"Have you asked them?"

"Well . . ." I stopped. "No."

That night over dinner, I asked my wife and children a question I didn't want to hear the answer to. "What do you think of the way I treat you?"

"You work a lot," my daughter said. "I wish we saw you more."

Looking back, I wish I had gone deeper with this answer. Today, I know there was so much more to understand. I didn't and couldn't. I only had duct tape and superglue as tools to fix things.

"Yeah, you're busy. I get it," my son said, "but I wish you had more time for us."

I began to hear the words from the famous song "Cat's in the Cradle." A boy wanted a father, and I gave him a warped idea of what a father should be to a son.

My wife sat across from me with "the look." Words weren't necessary; the silence was enough.

They were right—they'd been the last people on my priority list.

My wife grew up in a small town on the Ohio–Indiana border. Her brother and his wife would go to St. Mary's Lake for the weekends. We went with them one weekend, traveling down the narrow roads with corn and soybeans on each side. We stopped at a real country store full of candy bins, ice cream, and rows and rows of vegetables and fresh food. I thought I had walked onto *The Waltons* TV show.

We traveled back and forth together. Campfires, boating, and swimming in the lake. Days began to slow down. Laughter was not only something I heard; I became a part of that laughter. Locations don't make problems go away, but a change in location can change our perception, and the lake slowed me down.

So, over the summer, we bought a small cottage, and we stayed there every weekend for twenty-three years. Every time we made these trips, I could feel my blood pressure go down. It turns out you can do a lot of activities on a boat but working on your laptop or on a client file isn't one of them.

I began to see the small things in life. When we can see the small things, we realize they make the bigger things less important.

It's not all about success. It's about love. What better tool to repair my relationship with Victoria, my sales team, and the company? If caring about people worked for Dad, it could work for me. And since relationships are the currency of culture, it was about time to cash in on my inheritance of knowledge.

First, I had to cut my reading list down to zero. I didn't need another book. I had read so many books that I was confused. I can't imagine how confused others must have been.

Second, I had to get vulnerable with everyone around me, not just Victoria.

Third, I had to learn to care. Just care.

Remember the golden rule, "Do unto others as you would have them do unto you"? What about "Love your neighbor as yourself"? **Here's the problem**—*if you don't love yourself, your neighbor doesn't have a shot. The rest of the world doesn't, either.* I was so busy trying to impress people because I didn't love myself that I ended up hating myself and taking it out on everyone around me.

DESTRUCTIVE HERO REHAB

"If my dad built a company from nothing by having conversations with people about their lives," I told Pete, "maybe that will be enough for me, too."

"Maybe," Pete said. "Have you heard of the One Hundred Zero Principle?"

"The what?"

"It's the most effective way to create and sustain great relationships with others—both employees and family members. It goes like this." He drew a circle on the notepad in front of me. "You take full responsibility for the relationship. One hundred percent. And you expect nothing in return." He scribbled a tiny dot next to the circle. "Zero percent."

"Huh?"

"Implementing the One Hundred Zero Principle is not natural for most of us," Pete said. "It takes real commitment to think, act, and give one hundred percent."

"And a good dose of self-discipline."

"Correct." Pete nodded. "This may strike you as strange, but here's the paradox. When you take authentic responsibility for a relationship, more often than not, the other person chooses to take responsibility as well. Consequently, the One Hundred Zero relationship transforms into approaching one hundred to one hundred." Pete drew a second circle on the pad. "When that occurs, true breakthroughs happen for the individuals involved, plus their teams, their organizations, and their families."

"In other words, trade my expectation for appreciation, and the world changes instantly."

"Precisely, Scott."

"Note to self," I said. "Stop expecting. Start giving one hundred percent."

When I got back to the office that day, I walked around the company cubicles. I learned what our employees cared about outside of life at McGohan Brabender. Their favorite sports teams, their hobbies, their kids, and grandkids—I got curious about all of it. No hidden agenda. Just 100 percent responsibility on my part. And instead of telling people what *I* wanted them to do, think, feel, or say, I started *asking*.

A month into this Destructive Hero rehab, I called a team

meeting. Once everyone took their seats in the conference room, I opened with encouragement.

"We're doing well. No, *you* are doing well." I could tell from their folded arms they sensed a hidden agenda. "So well, in fact, that we need to hire a new person. Instead of writing the job description myself, I wanted to get your perspectives. What are some tasks you don't like to do around here?"

"I'm sorry . . . what?" one person piped up after an awkward silence.

"I'm serious. Think about all the tasks that are part of your job that you don't like doing, the things that don't give you energy. We'll turn your lists into a job description. Just imagine if we could find someone else to take care of those things! I think we could find someone who loves what we don't. We should try."

Victoria looked at me with a kind of smile that said, *You're beginning to get it.* Back then, I was just afraid my behavior and my speeding ticket from Victoria would be exposed. The other team members simply dropped their blank looks and began to write.

Ten minutes later, we had a job description, and two weeks later, we had a sixth person on our team. At the next team meeting, I made an even bigger ask.

"What would make your lives easier?"

"A four-day week!" someone said. "Can we have Fridays off?"

Well, I worked for an organization with more than forty people. I didn't have that kind of authority over forty, but I could try with the five people on our team.

"How about every fifth week?"

"Yes!"

So, every week, one team member got a Friday off. No more telling. Just asking.

I am not sure where my next question came from, but I do know it was an authentic question more than just trying to get out of trouble. These people meant a lot to me, and it was obvious they, too, were affected by my behavior. I honestly wanted it to be different. "Picture your perfect vacation," I said to everyone at the next meeting. Again, nothing to do with selling group insurance. "If you could go anywhere in the world, where would it be?"

"A cruise in Italy!" someone piped right up.

"I've always wanted to go to Hawaii," another said.

"OK. Done and done."

Silence. Everyone looked at one another, not quite sure if I meant what they hoped I did.

"I am not kidding. I am going to pay for each of your dream vacations. They're not going to count against your vacation days. And while each of you is gone, I'm going to make sure work doesn't stack up on your desks. We've got you covered."

"How—why? That's . . . wow . . . why?" One of our best employees teared up.

"Because it's about time I show you how much I care."

Every year, a member of the team had their dream vacation. And it was so much fun to put together! In the weeks leading up to their all-expenses-paid trip, every person doubled, if not tripled, their output. They had a blast working their tails off, and we had a blast reading the notes and postcards they sent while they were gone. Maybe my dad wasn't so crazy after all.

DO UNTO EMPLOYEES AS YOU WOULD
HAVE THEM DO UNTO YOU

The new hire, the Fridays off, the dream vacations—all of it came from one course-correcting conversation with Victoria. One hard-earned reward at a time, I got to see what an authentic employee experience looks like—a culture of people who love one another as *people*, not just as coworkers. For the first time, my relationships were authentic and built on mutual respect and admiration. We took care of one another because we cared about one another, and we were high performers the entire time.

Here's an exercise to help you better understand your employees.

When was the last time you stayed after work to walk around the cubicles? Do you know how your employees' parents are doing? Are they OK, or are they sick? Where do your managers' kids go to school? Do you have relationships with your people, or are you only concerned about their role in your company? This experience applies to small and large organizations. Simply begin to understand your team, the people closest to you. In an increasingly virtual world, this will become even more important because you can now look into their world at home and see the little things that matter to them. **Learn what is important to your people, and you can reset your ability to inspire each other.**

Some leaders have access to employees' addresses. This may appear to be intrusive, so I will leave it up to you. If you want a different view, look one up. Drive by their house, and take a moment to view the world through their lens. Think about the example you see at work. Are you shoving your work ethic, good or bad, down the throats of your people? In other words, are you working fifty, sixty, seventy hours a week and expecting others to do the same?

After your office is closed for the day, walk around your employees' workspaces and look at what's important to your people. You'll see it in pictures, knickknacks, sports memorabilia, and inspirational quotes, to name a few. You probably won't find a picture of your building or your leadership team.

Believe it or not, maintaining good relationships is so much easier than command and control. And it's free, not counting any dream vacations. You don't have to pacify your employees—or your family—with the latest gadgets to show them you care. As I worked my way up to CEO of the company, I tried to instill these habits into every team leader. I made mistakes (and still do!), but at least these mistakes came from a place of virtue instead of arrogance.

Leaders who've worn the Destructive Hero cape and mask fear a culture of love. Actually, your fear of love could very well be the lack of love you have for yourself. *Remember, the mirror is a wonderful place to find a friend. Be a friend to yourself, and you can begin to be a friend to others.*

Caring about your employees first and profitability second seems like a problem if you've done culture, employee engagement, and employee experience the way popular books, state-of-the-art training programs, and highly paid coaches teach. That's how you end up with a culture that makes your top performer quit—or worse, go to prison! Remember Enron?

Good people let bad companies torque their values. At Enron and other fallen organizations, nobody piped up and said, "That's not right, and I know it's not right," when it counted. But in a culture where mutual appreciation, understanding, and respect are the reference points, nobody gets away with that crap.

Build a culture that rests in nobility. That's the kind of culture I want to create. Because that's the kind of culture where I want to work.

Reflection: Let's Go Inside

Remember the triangle (page 17)? What words did you hear or what words did you tell yourself are true and what words are lies?

Example: Words that are true: I am kind.
Words that are lies: I am not creative.

How have the lies you told yourself created an identity that is not who you are or want to be?

Remember the poetry example? What did you love doing as a child that you stopped because society told you a lie?

Example: When I was little, I loved to draw,
but others we better, so I told myself I wasn't
good enough.

What are the words you desire to hear from others?

Example: You are humble.
You are kind.
You are considerate.

Instead of desiring these words from others, would you consider giving them away to people you know?
Who are they?
Will you find them?
Will you tell them?

CHAPTER 3

The Culture Gap

Several years ago, I took my family to a company event. Like all parents, we hoped our kids would behave and make us proud. Sadly, we often expect our children to behave at the grocery store, church, and the park, yet we tolerate bad behavior inside our own homes. Inconsistent expectations result in a gap between what we ask of our children at home and what we expect of them when we go out. Maybe that's because we, the adults, have our own behavior gaps.

My behavior changed at that event—as if someone had flipped an "ego on" switch. I wanted to make sure I said hello to everyone. Rather, I wanted *everyone to know I was there*. It sucks to admit it, but it's the truth. All I cared about was my reputation.

On the way home, the kids were tired. So was I. Away from the crowd, I flipped back to my previous behavior. It didn't go unnoticed.

"Dad, can we stop at McDonald's for a Happy Meal?" my daughter, Courtney, asked. "Please?"

"No," I said. "It's getting late. I'm tired. We're going home."

"But, Dad!"

"No!"

"You were so nice a few minutes ago. Why are you so grumpy all of a sudden?"

My wife didn't say a word. As a matter of fact, she didn't even look at me. I caught her raising her eyebrows as if to say, *I hope he heard that one.* And I did. Courtney called out the gap between who I wanted people to think I was and who I actually was.

Just like my behavior that evening, a company's culture is often at odds with its reputation. So how do you reconcile that gap? The first step is to be honest about your culture. That's a taller order than you might expect!

CULTURE ≠ REPUTATION

Most leaders don't know they have a culture until they realize it's broken, and it's too late. **Cultures are hard to build and much harder to repair, but easy to destroy.** Just like trust, you acquire it in drips and lose it in buckets. I know because I nearly destroyed mine. Before Victoria pushed me to reform my Destructive Hero ways, I was as guilty of misunderstanding culture as that CEO in my class. He believed his organization didn't have a culture, but I hadn't even known what culture was!

Like a lot of leaders, I got caught up in organizational performance—the balance sheet, payroll, books about high-performing organizations, stock prices, and today's edition of *The Wall Street Journal.* I assumed culture was synonymous with reputation. Reputation is what your workforce and your customers think about you. Or in some cases, what you *hope* they think about you. That's why I pushed myself and our team members to work longer hours and expected them to consider their values second to their performance.

It turns out a lot of leaders make the same assumption I did. When leaders ask me during the Course for Presidents Q&A how I nurture McGohan Brabender's culture of mutual appreciation, understanding, and respect, their questions imply that building (or fixing) a *culture* is the same as managing (or repairing) their *reputation*. Even when leaders *do* commit to fixing a broken culture, their action plans that emerge often say nothing about character, relationships, or company values. Instead, they're littered with bullet points about reputation, rebranding, and catchy PR headlines.

As a result, they approach the five senses of culture (more on this later) with commands, not questions. Too many leaders sold their souls to the press long ago, so they tell their people what they *should* see, feel, hear, taste, and smell. Whatever it takes to earn that five-star reputation!

"We're a company of open doors. When our employees look around, that's all they see. Everyone, from our direct reports to the interns, feels like their work matters. They feel like they're making a real difference," they say . . . while compensation across the organization remains slightly below market average due to the antiquated compensation structure of the industry.

"I'm open to our employees' feedback. Hearing from people is critical to sustained success," they say, while leadership meets behind closed doors.

"Life at our company is fresh and satisfying. You can practically taste the results!" they say, while entire departments saunter in ten minutes late and sneak out ten minutes early every single day.

"We believe in authentic leadership at all levels. We're the real deal, or at least we try, and our people can smell it," they say, while employees gossip about ulterior motives and hidden agendas.

When you think having a great culture only means having

a great reputation, it's more important to *tell* everyone your culture is world-class than to *make* your culture world-class. Personal branding first, truth telling second. My journey taught me to lead by example.

Culture is about character, not reputation. Reputation is branding and perception; character is relationships and the values that guard those relationships. Reputation is outside in; character is inside out. Reputation tells; character asks.

Reputation-driven leaders pressure people to improve. If they don't, they're "downsized." But nobody likes pressure, so that tactic isn't effective. Character-driven leaders get vulnerable instead. Excellent culture, in its truest sense, *is* vulnerability. People feel safe enough to say, "I need help," when needed. And they *get* help. No matter what, they know they're not alone. They feel together. *That's* a world-class culture.

Unfortunately, a lot of leaders shy away from being vulnerable. If you have a vision or a dream, you're supposed to appear strong and bold to get your dreams in the air. That's how it works. I can understand why. When you start an organization, you have many fears you feel on the pillow at night, alone and afraid. Society, banks, investors, and employees have expectations of resilience and authority. Entrepreneurs can pull this off. Most often, we have no other choice.

This attitude creates a mask of ego and pride that's difficult to remove. You see, this attitude of success has carried us far. Why would showing anyone our innermost fear work when faking it works?

At McGohan Brabender, we believe that customers, investors, and banks all expect this attitude from a leader. We *think* employees expect the same, but they don't. Great leaders know that being vulnerable might be the greatest trait of all. When you are vulnerable, you let people know they are not alone.

Everyone has problems. Most of our problems are upstairs in our heads. Society tells us to always look bold and strong, and people will follow. Society is wrong. People love under-dogs because most people see themselves as underdogs. They won't fight for themselves, but they will fight for others. The beauty arises when they see vulnerability come alive, and they transfer it to their own lives.

A leader who is tough and bold enough to share their weakness lets others know that it's OK to be vulnerable. A leader who is clear about the problems in front of them and vulnerable enough to say they do not have all the answers will create a creative learning culture of employees who want to solve a problem. They will solve the issue in front of them for the leader and for the customers and the business!

I have had people tell me my vulnerability is a weakness. They might be the most broken of all. They are paralyzed in their own mess and problems and mask them all in perfection.

I have seen the benefits of vulnerability. It makes us human. A pursuit of perfection is miserable for others and a terrible goal to strive for. Again, nothing is worse than being around someone who thinks they are perfect. Progress is a beautiful destination, and it's the only one we should strive for, together.

WHAT EXACTLY IS CHARACTER?

Keep this in mind: If you choose reputation at the expense of character when building your culture, you'll get neither. When you pour your energies into building character rather than reputation, you get both. Think about the greatest brands or organizations you've ever experienced. Walt Disney? Ritz-Carlton? Nordstrom? Their cultures didn't happen by accident. Their reputations are the result of a commitment to excellence and employee empowerment. They enrich their employees' lives, and employees, in turn, enrich the business.

For example, before Walt Disney World opened, Walt had all the carousel horses coated in twenty-four-karat-gold paint. The customers never knew it, but the employees did. The employees took care of them like they *were* gold. As a result, the customers never saw a dirty carousel. Disney reversed the psychology of taking care of customers. If he wanted the carousels taken care of with excellence, he could have mandated cleanliness. He didn't. He painted them with a precious metal, and that alone inspired employees to clean the precious carousels. Beautifully done, Walt! Get your employee experience right, and your customer experience falls right into line. In a culture of character, employees treat customers the way they want to be treated—because *you* treat your employees the way *they* want to be treated.

So, what exactly *is* character? **Character has many shapes, but it will often come alive when things get tough.** Downsizing, deaths, and market pressures are common examples. Do employers comfort their laid-off employees and help carry boxes to their cars, or do they escape the office on spontaneous vacations? Do your people pitch in to order flowers for the funeral, or do they shrug it off because grief is messy and they've got a business to run? Do you warn your staff about upcoming industry disruptions and ask for their advice, or do you keep them in the dark because they might freak out?

MORE THAN PING-PONG TABLES

Close your eyes and imagine walking through your building. Think about what you see and how it makes you feel. What your employees see when they come to work is important, but even more important is how they *feel* when they see it. I'd rather be surrounded by people who care about me as a person than by company-sponsored yoga balls and Ping-Pong tables. Is a Ping-Pong table better than working with someone who takes the time to ask about your weekend?

Just as culture isn't about perks, it should *never* be about profitability. If yours is a culture of character and love, where relationships drive high performance, people shouldn't have to worry that mutual appreciation, understanding, and respect change based on the company's profitability.

Between reputation and character lies a Grand Canyon. Don't get me wrong: reputation matters. There's an entire industry for it—reputation management! But if you want a reputation as a state-of-the-art company, you have to build that reputation from the inside out, and that *starts* with your character. And in turn, your character starts with your values.

To define our values, we didn't tell our employees what our values were (I'd tried that before!), and we didn't hire a consultant to come up with a values statement that sounded like a fast-food commercial jingle. No, we invited all seventy-five employees into a room and *asked* them.

"Our company values are important," I announced to the overstuffed conference room. "So . . . what are they? What are some of the things you think we should care about?"

"We care about each other. We're like a family," someone in HR said.

"Great. 'Family.' What does that mean?"

We would need more than half a dozen follow-up meetings to unpack that single word. "Family," our employees ultimately decided, "encompasses our homes, our workplace, and our community."

I agree. The business comes second. If our number one value is family, then we put people first in every decision we make, every customer we serve, and every new employee we onboard. With family first, the number one goal of McGohan Brabender's culture is to grow better fathers and mothers, husbands and wives, men and women. The company *cannot* help but benefit as a result. And it makes MB a fun place to work! If nobody has to drag themselves to work on Monday morning, our community is a much better place.

Home, community, workplace—in that order. If our motive as an employer is to create an environment that betters our people, we benefit from better employees. And the community benefits, too. Of course, we have to actually live up to our values. Otherwise, you get an office full of Victorias who know their leaders are hypocrites!

YOU MIGHT BE LYING TO YOURSELF

I met one CEO who told me his primary company value was compassion. I thought that was interesting, and from the way he spoke, I became curious about what compassion meant to him and his company. I asked him why, and I was ready for an incredible answer. He had a lot of energy and spoke with passion. I had a mindset that we believed in the same life values, the same purpose.

"Well, compassion matters. We're all about giving back, and I care about my business. But long-term, I want to grow my business so I can sell it."

Sell it, that's interesting, then what? I was hoping for a better answer, but . . . nothing.

Simply: "I want to sell it, buy a boat, and build a home in Hilton Head."

That guy lied to himself. Compassion is *not* a value at his company! Don't get me wrong, you're allowed to sell your company. That's capitalism. So if that's you, your culture should be wrapped around words like *progress . . . innovation . . . growth oriented.*

That CEO should tell his people, "When you work hard,

you're going to be rewarded." That's honest. What's not honest is pretending you want to give back. No, you don't. You want to build valuation. You want to get rich. There's nothing wrong with that—a lot of people want to work in an organization that values performance-based rewards. You'll find passionate people who love your company. But be honest with your employees. You can't claim to walk on both sides of the street and still maintain a good culture.

VOICE MAILS, GOLF, AND TELLING THE TRUTH

One year, we had a compensation shift for our sales staff. Our compensation level was one of the highest in the industry, and it was set for both owners (shareholders) and nonowners. Our shift would impact everyone. We decided to shift the throttle down, and in a rush, I recorded a voice mail to send to the shareholders to let them know. Instead, I sent the voice mail to the *entire* company. Ouch!

I tried everything, from calling IT to running around pulling every phone off the hook. The only way to delete the voice mail was to delete *every* voice mail from every employee. That would mean every customer request and every special voice mail saved would be lost. I knew that was not an option. My only option was the truth. So, I went to work on another voice mail, unpacking our decision and explaining my mistake. Nobody said an honest culture was easy. I wanted to take the path of least resistance and avoid what was hard. I was embarrassed, and I didn't want to own up to this publicly. It was a natural response. I have learned that when I lean into things I don't want to do and am even scared to do, I move forward and grow. Every time when the truth—not *my* truth—is the quest, we all win. I like to say there are only three things that don't lie—little kids, drunk people, and yoga pants. The rest of us have to try harder.

Even if you don't think you have a culture, you *do* have one. And it might not be as bad as you fear. The only way to find out is to get honest with yourself and your people. Sure, it can be embarrassing. A few years ago, I told a story publicly for the first time—the most embarrassing story of my life.

Every year, I take part in a summer program for inner-city students called Worth It, Why Mentors Matter. For eight weeks, we team up forty inner-city kids with forty adult leaders. Now, what does a forty-nine-year-old, tie-wearing guy have in common with an inner-city kid? Quite frankly, I don't know. But I do know that, as a young kid, my life was filled with low self-worth. Fear, ego, and pride created a dysfunctional, delusional Scott—and I held onto that person for decades. But over time, I realized leadership has a lot more to do with humility and vulnerability than with being smart or charismatic.

A few years ago, I was scheduled to speak to the students about integrity. I got up the courage to share this story. I didn't want to—which I knew meant that I should.

When I was fourteen years old, I played in a golf tournament at the golf course that my dad belonged to. It was a junior golf tournament—a bunch of boys and girls competing for a trophy. I cheated to beat a girl named Sue. I know. Not a proud moment. I still had the trophy in my basement in an old, beat-up box. It haunted me, but I'd learned to get past my fear and move toward change.

The day I told this story to the high schoolers, I brought the trophy with me. I thought having it in my hand would make my lesson come alive.

"If you make a mistake like this, don't use your past to torture yourself," I told them. "Use your past to be useful and helpful to other people."

Right in the middle of my presentation, Rhonda, a freshman, interrupted me. "Coach Scott," she said, standing up, "that's not your trophy, that's *hers*. You need to give it back."

"I don't use my past to torture myself. I use my past to be useful to others," I said.

"Thank you. I get that. But the trophy isn't yours. You need to give it back."

I tried to continue my talk, but she wouldn't let me.

"Coach Scott, you have to do the right thing. You have to give it back." She wasn't rude or disrespectful—she was simply honest.

"Rhonda, you're right. Tell you what: I'll try to find Sue before the end of the summer so I can give the trophy to its rightful owner."

"Good. Thank you," she said.

I went home that night with that terrible trophy. Over the next few days, I didn't try very hard to find Sue. But that weekend, during my next round of golf, I was chatting with the golf pro, an old friend. I told him the story and what Rhonda had said. He laughed.

"What's so funny?"

"I know Sue. Her brother's my next-door neighbor."

"Oh . . . wow. I don't believe God has coincidences for any of us, but . . ."

"Let me give you his number so you can get in touch with Sue."

Fantastic. I was in it now. I called Sue's brother and asked him how I could get in touch with his sister.

"Why do you need to reach Sue?"

Seriously? I thought about lying. But I sighed and told him the story—the cheating, Rhonda's challenge, my golf pro friend. He laughed.

"Have you any idea what my sister does now?"

"No."

"She's the women's golf coach at the University of South Florida."

"You're kidding me."

"I'll give you the athletic director's number."

I took it, called him, and finally got Sue on the phone.

"I remember you," she said.

"Well, I'm doing this inner-city program for students, and this freshman Rhonda had the courage to call me out. I was telling a story about that junior golf tournament that you and I played in."

"Ah, yes. I remember."

"Yes, well, uh . . ." This was much harder than I'd thought it would be. "The thing is, well, I cheated. I still remember walking past you and your parents, carrying the trophy in my hand at dinner. Anyway, technically, I have *your* trophy . . . from over thirty years ago. And Rhonda encouraged me to find you and give it back. Actually, she was relentless about it. So, I'm trying to do the right thing."

"Holy cow."

"Did you sense that I had cheated?"

"No, I didn't. But cheating in high school and middle school golf happens all the time."

"It doesn't make it right," I said.

"Can I tell this story to my college students? I'm dealing with a similar situation."

"Sure. Actually, could I pay for you to fly back to Dayton? I'd love to give you this trophy in front of Rhonda."

"Well, I'm in the middle of recruiting right now. But I know my mom remembers you. I know she'd love to honor you and Rhonda. She could come accept it on my behalf."

Oh, this is getting better and better.

All said and done, we held an event at the golf club to give Sue's mom the trophy. Rhonda had no idea what was coming. A hundred people showed up, including the mayor, the police chief, the media, friends, colleagues, and my whole family. Talk about embarrassing.

I had a speech to read and the trophy to present to Sue's mom. I got up to the podium and started reading. My lips quivered. *I can't do this.*

Rhonda must have seen me struggling. She stood up, walked to the podium, and put her arm around me. "Coach Scott, let's do this together."

And we did. I made it—we made it. Together.

Right after I gave Sue's mom the trophy, she handed me a bigger trophy—a bronze caddie helping a younger golfer line up a putt.

"You didn't earn the first trophy. You stole it. But this one you earned."

If ever there's a fire in my office building, I'm not leaving without grabbing that trophy.

Because of Rhonda, I began to know Scott from the inside out. I'm grateful that, despite our difference of age, race, gender, and title, Rhonda wasn't afraid to call me out. That summer, she taught me more than I taught her.

I received two rewards that day: the trophy from Sue's mom and the lesson Rhonda gave me. I treasure them both more than you know.

EVERYONE HAS A CULTURE (AND A CULTURE GAP)

Remember, character drives values, which drive culture— pretty simple. The truth is so important—but be careful to look for the *right* truth. Many of us can get caught up in "our truth." That is the story we tell ourselves or others who won't or can't be honest with us. We tell ourselves these truths, and they become "the truth" to us. It is not "the truth," it's "our truth," and that work is hard and worth every drop of sweat and every tear.

To explore the gaps in your personal culture and your organization's culture and find "the truth" about both, create a culture where your employees treat your people and your customers like gold. Start by fixing the culture you already have. Set the example. Start with *your* character. You might get a trophy out of it.

Reflection: Let's Go Inside

1. What are the gaps in your personal culture?
2. What do you want people to say about you? What would they say today?
3. What are you willing to do to make this different in your life?
4. What are the gaps in your organization's culture? Where is it today? Where could it be?
5. Who can change it?
6. Will you? Why? Why not?

CHAPTER 4

Culture Blind Spots

On the outskirts of Tipp City, Ohio, tucked among an over-grown prairie, a small pond, and a hidden waterfall, sits the world-class campus of Aileron. After selling his business and sharing proceeds of the sale with employees, Clay Mathile, the former CEO and owner of the IAMS Company, opened Aileron, a nonprofit institution where private business leaders teach their peers how to manage their workforce, create more jobs in their communities, and perpetuate their organizations to the next generation.

I was lucky enough to cofacilitate Aileron's flagship program, the Course for Presidents, a few times. I shared my father's high-performance-culture insights with executives and presidents from all over Ohio and the United States. I would usually spend the first half of the full-day class listening and the second half speaking about culture and answering questions.

Usually.

During the most recent iteration of the course, a local CEO stood up right in the middle of my presentation and crossed his arms.

"I don't *have* a culture, and I don't *need* one." He sounded like a three-year-old staring down a plate full of broccoli.

I'm a volunteer at Aileron, not a paid staff member, so I can say whatever I want without risking anything. Well . . . *almost* whatever I want.

"OK, fine," I said. "As an owner and entrepreneur, you have the right to not *want* a culture. But you *do* have one."

"But I don't!" he insisted, sitting down.

I smirked. "Show of hands, everyone," I said to the thirty or so leaders. "Who here thinks this person has a culture?"

Every single hand went up.

My stubborn friend shot to his feet again. "No way! My company does *not* have a culture!"

"Trust me. You do," I said. "You're showing it to me right now."

When the class ended, he apologized for his behavior and told me he was going to sell the company anyway. A good choice for humanity!

WHAT'S IT LIKE TO WORK FOR YOUR COMPANY?

Jockeys put blinders on their racehorses to keep them focused on the race. Many leaders, including me, have had the luxury of blinders while being oblivious to the consequences of wearing them. These blinders create blind spots. Why don't we do something about them? Well, they're called blind spots for a reason—we can't see them! Or we choose not to.

If you listen to your past, you might hear people trying to tell you about these blind spots. Do you recall how you resisted their feedback?

Remember the song "Cat's in the Cradle"? It tells the story of a man who never kept his promises to his son. When I heard those lyrics as a kid, I promised myself I wouldn't be *that* guy, *that* parent, *that* husband. But guess what? I *did* become that guy, that parent, that husband. I broke that promise. People told me along the way—I just didn't want to hear it.

My father said to me, "Your grandfather told me not to burn the candle at both ends."

I didn't take the hint.

My wife asked me, "Why does all this *stuff* matter so much?"

"Don't you see how hard I work?" I shot back, dodging her question. *Look at everything I provide for this family.* I did not say this line, but it was pounding in my head. I wanted to say so many other things. I thought, *They are the selfish ones; I am working my tail off for them.* Looking back now at my previous self, I think, *What a jerk. What a lie.*

My grandmother asked me, "What's going on, Scott?"

"Nothing. I'm busy. I'm doing a lot of great things."

"I'm impressed," she said. "And I want to encourage you to look deeper into a relationship with a loving God."

I never listened. Not to the advice, anyway. I *did* hear the applause.

"Wow, I can't believe everything you've accomplished!"

"That's a cool car!"

"You went *where* on vacation? That sounds amazing!"

Those words were fuel to my fire. I was drunk on my blinders and deaf to the words of wisdom.

If you want to, you *can* see the truth of your destructive behaviors and their consequences. Then you can do something about them! But only if you're honest with yourself. The CEO of Campbell Soup once said, "You can't act your way out of something you behaved your way into. You can only behave your way out."

Sometimes, the best way to find a blind spot is to look at it from another person's perspective. I'd like you to imagine the following scene with me: You're at a neighborhood barbecue, and one of your employees is there too. You smell the hamburgers and the hot dogs sizzling on the grill. A breeze whips a few plastic plates off the checkered tablecloth. Kids play pick-up baseball a few yards away from the picnic shelter. You see your employee's hand reach deep into an icy cooler. Someone walks up to her and makes casual conversation.

"So, what's it like to work at your company?"

What does your employee say about your organization? She can't see you. She doesn't know you're there listening, so she's honest. No filter. Nothing at stake. What does she say? More importantly, what do you *want* her to say?

Then her acquaintance asks her about *you*, the one in charge.

What do you want her to say? And what does she *actually* say? If you answer each question differently, that's your chasm—the distance between where your culture is and where it should be. For some organizations (and their leaders), it's a tiny crack. For others, it's a giant gap between two mountains with no crossing bridge in sight.

THE FOUR CULTURAL BEHAVIORS

If corruption starts at the top and works its way down the organizational hierarchy, so does *reformation*. Even in the most cohesive cultures, you'll find four types of cultural behaviors. The first three are victims, naysayers, and bystanders—people who once believed in your organization but have had their values torqued one, two, or ten too many times. The fourth type is who you are looking for—the believers!

Don't get me wrong, we are not trying to turn a culture into a cult. I have learned 20 percent of the people will do exactly as you asked, 20 percent will not do anything you asked, and if they do, they will deliver half of the results. It's the 60 percent in the middle we are trying to steer in a new direction—better clarity and a vision they can get behind.

If you have victims, naysayers, or bystanders lurking around your office, chances are high they'll voice all their frustrations about you when someone at the neighborhood picnic asks. Especially after a cold beer or two! Do you recognize them?

Victims say things like, "I can't believe this is happening," and "Nobody cares," when problems arise. They withdraw to their offices, cubicles, or projects. They challenge the organization's direction, and they don't like progress.

Naysayers are the opposite. They toss in their two cents without being asked and act like they wrote a $1,000 check. "This place isn't what it used to be," you'll hear them whine. Maybe they're right, but they never offer *constructive* criticism. Theirs is resentful, entitled criticism that deflates everyone around them.

While naysayers get their hands dirty making a mess even worse, bystanders watch from the sidelines, waiting for the clock to strike five. When you announce your plans to improve company culture, they'll assume it's a new management fad, like the book-of-the-month club last year. "I'm too busy," bystanders say. "Not my job."

If you recognize these behaviors in your organization, your culture needs serious repair. That's the bad news. The good news is that where victims, naysayers, and bystanders can be found, so can believers. Believers remember the good times. They cherish the company's values. Believers energize everyone in a meeting and say, "Let's try it! We've been successful before. We'll be successful again." Believers know that victims, naysayers, and bystanders can change. So can the Destructive Heroes whose behavior made employees so cynical in the first place.

That doesn't mean it's easy to reform victims, naysayers, and bystanders. But when you *do* reform them, they're your company's biggest advocates. And when you imagine them at the barbecue, you know exactly what they'll say about your company, your culture, and you. And you'll love what you hear.

The truth can hurt, but it *will* set you free. Your victims, naysayers, and bystanders are there for a reason. As leaders, we owe them. The majority of their behavior could be our fault for not having crucial conversations with them. We've never addressed their issues, and that lacks dignity.

WHAT DO YOU SEE IN YOUR BLIND SPOT?

Sometimes I am asked to speak about the five senses of culture at a workshop for local business owners, presidents, or human resources personnel. Inside of that workshop, I facilitate an exercise that provokes people to think differently about themselves and their organizations. I encourage them to pretend by using their sense of smell, their thoughts, and the beauty of silence. I ask them to imagine they're watching and listening to the fun and the conversations surrounding the barbecue. They can hear the sounds of laughter, ice shifting when a hand reaches into a cooler, birds, and the summer breeze running through the trees.

You begin to watch someone who works with you, and they are speaking to another person in your organization. This second person asks your employee questions about what they are doing and how it is going. And then the question comes out of their mouth: "You work closely with _____. What are they like?"

You want them to say great things about you. How you inspire them and encourage them. Maybe how clear you are when you delegate and how you have helped them grow into an amazing person. That may be what you want to hear, but you don't hear it. What you hear is the raw truth.

The secret in this process is to get honest with yourself and begin to explore the blind spots. These spots are your perceptions about your ability to lead—a person, a group, and maybe even your family.

Remember the difference between "your truth" and "the truth." That's the honest place you're trying to find.

I believe what someone once told me: "You can't fix something that is broken with something that is broken." If your perception about yourself and others is broken, you can't fix it. If you begin to honestly unpack where and why it's broken, you are well on your way.

Now, this is not a place for you to beat yourself up. We are all human and make mistakes, but we don't have to continue to make them—*if* we understand and know what they are.

During the Q&A, more than one attendee has asked for clarification on this exercise.

"How do I know what my employee would say?"

"What if I think I have a great culture, but it's actually terrible? Or vice versa?"

"How do you determine what steps to take to close a blind spot?"

Not only are they unsure of the answers, but they also don't have the first clue how to find them. Maybe you know how they feel! **That gap between the employee's *honest* answer and the *ideal* answer is a blind spot.** Blind spots usually indicate leadership's character defects. Why? Because as the leaders go, so goes the culture.

I call them blind spots because you can't see them. You can't measure them. And if you can't measure them, you can't manage them . . . or repair them. Right? Wrong—you can.

I didn't intend to wound Victoria with the way I behaved, but I did. I thought I was an attentive, caring father, but I wasn't. I was worse than flying blind—I was *living* blind. That didn't bode well for McGohan Brabender, my family, friends, or humanity.

TRUTH TELLERS AND GRUDGES

If you're going to build a quality culture (or repair the one you already have), you're going to have to do the hard, hard, hard work of identifying your blind spots *yourself.* Unless you're lucky enough to work with a Victoria, those closest to you probably won't give you the honest feedback they would have no trouble sharing with a random stranger at a neighborhood picnic.

For example, if you have older kids, imagine sitting down on their bed and asking, "Hey, what do you think my blind spots are? Where am I messing up but I have no clue I'm messing up?" What would they say? They're playing on their iPhone. They're jingling their car keys. It's allowance day, and they're thinking about their big date tonight. Any truth they *would* tell you is choked by their financial, social, and relational ties to you.

Even if you ask your employees directly, they will hesitate to spill the beans on what it's *really* like to work at your company. I don't care what their role is—if you're responsible for signing their checks or have any leverage over them, their team, or their department, it limits their ability to be frank.

My blind spot—that I'd rather be liked than trusted— made a lot of sales, but who knows how many potential clients I turned away from the company? Once Victoria shined her spotlight on it, I had a choice. I could keep behaving the way I always had, or I could start representing the company's stated values. Most leaders never get that chance. When their culture is in trouble, they don't do anything about it.

Do you have a truth teller in your organization? By the grace of God, Victoria is still with McGohan Brabender. She is a truth teller! Beth Ferrin, our CFO, is also my truth teller.

Mike Suttman, our president, is also a truth teller for me. Sometimes, he will tell people he is my sandbag. Often I go to the clouds and need to be pulled back to earth. He does this for me with respect and a friendship that is dear to me.

My wife and I have authentic conversations about how we were raised. What our beliefs are, where they came from, and how we feel about them today. I adore my wife, and she is my best friend because we treat each other like best friends. She is my hero, my truth teller, and my counselor.

This is my belief: When we don't get our way or we have been offended emotionally and don't address these issues quickly, they turn into resentment. Resentment is the number one offender in most relationships. If you let those resentments stack up in your life, you will leak. For example, you might get into an argument over someone being late to a meeting, and the anger is really tilted toward a project that was late. You will leak against yourself, your family, and others—but often *not* against the person, place, or thing that let you down. Truth tellers help you work through situations with honesty, humility, and empathy. I am grateful for all of my truth tellers.

Maybe your culture needs repair, too. If so, it got into its state of *disrepair* because of blind spots a few people saw but said nothing about.

Have you ever used your temper to keep others in line? Maybe you haven't realized it, and they never told you. Maybe there's a good reason you get red-hot so quickly. When you were little, something bad happened, and anger protected you. The madder you got, the safer you felt.

Maybe your blind spot is sarcasm. Your people can't tell a joke from a dig or a compliment from an underhanded insult. But since no one has ever told you how a remark made them feel, how would you know? Exactly. You wouldn't. Because it's a blind spot. That's why the employee experience program you invested in hasn't improved performance, why the latest round of wellness perks HR announced went unclaimed, and why you dread reading your company's anonymous Glassdoor reviews. On the outside, your company looks like a great place to work. But inside, employees walk around with unspoken grudges. I've seen it a hundred times.

These grudges hold your company back from becoming everything it can be. As a leader, you express your company's values by how you treat your people. If one of your company's values is friendliness, but you're not friendly, you'll have yourself an office full of grudges. You don't realize you're a liar, but that's exactly what your employee at the barbecue will tell her friend. You *want* to be nice. You *think* you're trustworthy. You *try* to be friendly. But your intentions won't show up in her answers. Only your behaviors will.

I often see this on the golf course. When everything is going well, it's all smiles and grins, but when it's not going well, it's a potluck as to who will show up. One of my best friends, Charlie McMahan, is a pastor of a large church in Dayton, Ohio. He loves golf, and we've played together a few times with complete strangers. They have no idea he is a pastor, so the language and shenanigans are wide open and in full view. Often, during a round, the conversation comes up about what each of us does for a living. I always appreciate the look on their faces when they find out he is a pastor. The rest of the round feels like a bro love fest.

To transform your culture, you can't *say* you're changing things around the office. Like writing *integrity* on your wall. You have to *prove* you've changed. Shine a light on those blind spots. Close that culture gap. Maybe that means giving your employees every fifth Friday off. At the very least, give your employees the authentic you. If you're not honest with your people and yourself, how can you learn where your blind spots are in the future?

A CULTURE IN TROUBLE

Think about Wells Fargo, the stagecoach company turned up-side down. In the book *Good to Great: Why Some Companies Make the Leap . . . and Others Don't,* management expert Jim Collins praises Wells Fargo as an elite organization with a bright future. Eight years later, Collins released a follow-up book, *How the Mighty Fall and Why Some Companies Never Give In,* to explain how "great" companies like Wells Fargo destroy their own reputations. Here's what happened.

In 2016, Wells Fargo was fined $250 million for opening unauthorized checking accounts and credit cards on behalf of their customers and for overcharging homeowners for appraisals. For anyone who asks, I think Wells Fargo is a good company. They lost their way quickly and jeopardized a historical brand. I don't believe for a second that all 269,000 Wells Fargo employees were responsible for the company's fall. I think it started with one person who allowed someone to open a customer credit card they hadn't requested. How do you think co-workers felt when that person came in the next day driving a brand-new car and wearing a brand-new outfit?

I want some of that, too, they thought. *They're not getting in trouble.* And many others in the workforce followed.

The Consumer Financial Protection Bureau caught up to their antics. In all, 5,300 people lost their jobs. I doubt all of them were bad people. A culture in trouble *gets* into trouble because one person—the leader—doesn't live up to the company's values, excusing everyone else from doing so, too. At Wells Fargo, the person in charge of defrauding customers walked away with nearly $60 million in compensation, even after penalties. A $60 million *reward* for destroying the finances of all those customers? What sort of message does that send to employees? Especially the over five thousand people who lost their jobs? If that's not a culture in trouble, I don't know what is.

WHAT YOU TOLERATE, YOU ENCOURAGE

How do you reform your victims, naysayers, and bystanders into believers? How do you know for sure what they will say to their friends about you and your company when you're not there?

Get truthful with your people. Have clear, honest conversations with them about what your business needs now and in the future, what *they* need to make that happen, and how you can manage and measure their progress. What you tolerate, you encourage.

What will you tolerate? Try tolerating love. It's a word we don't use much in the workforce, but it's a word most people adore. This is what love means to McGohan Brabender:

L—Learn. We learn so much by listening to others. God gave us two ears for a reason.

O—Observe. Watching others helps us understand people. We rarely learn anything while our mouths are running.

V—Vulnerability. Human connection plus truth equals vulnerability. Sharing our own faults lets others know they are not alone.

E—Encourage. It's like my father said a long time ago: "Everyone needs encouragement, and the people that deserve it the least need it the most."

Love is the oldest gift we have. The easiest way to start showing your people you care is to have a crucial conversation. Ask open-ended questions, then listen. Remember, you don't need to have the answers. You are on a quest to identify problems. Asking and listening are not about fixing; they're about understanding.

The major difference between a crucial conversation and the most common alternative, a confrontation, is *who* the conversation is about. When you confront an employee, your perspective is that their behavior is all about *you*. I've overheard many Destructive Heroes berate low-performing employees, and it always makes me cringe.

"Do you have any idea how your behavior reflects upon me? I have sales goals, and you're not helping me meet them. You're supposed to do your job!"

If a previously reliable employee falls into a slump, sometimes it has nothing to do with you. Unfortunately, there's this thing called life, and it kicks people in the ass. Nine times out of ten, that gossiper, drama queen, backstabber, or sarcastic pessimist in your organization got that way because life outside of work isn't shaping up how they wanted. No one has taught them to deal with life on life's terms. Maybe they have a sick, elderly parent or a rebellious teenager at home. Maybe their student loan payments bite off most of their paycheck, and they can't save for a future.

Give your victims, naysayers, and bystanders a place to talk and be heard. No, you're not your employees' life coach. But you want measurable results. To get those results, you need positive relationships with the people in charge of producing those results (your employees). And to build those relationships, you need to invest time. I'm not talking hours per day, just a few minutes here and there.

For example, I recently heard an employee complain to his

team lead about a new company policy. "I've always done it the old way," he said, among other choice words.

Time for a crucial conversation, I thought. This naysayer was doing a good job because he was still working for our company. But people can get set in their ways—and then get stuck in them.

I called our disgruntled employee into my office about an unrelated matter. A few minutes in, I changed the subject.

"Between you and me, I'm a little worried about you. Your performance in the past has been great, but I'm not seeing you in your natural state these days. What's going on? I'm here to listen."

"It's that new model you have us following. I don't like it," he shot back. "I've always done it the old way. It's worked for years. I like the old way."

"OK, I'm not disagreeing with you," I said. "The problem isn't you, me, or somebody down the hall. The problem is that we're one hundred and eighty-five people across four locations. I respect and admire the work you've done. But if we're going to sustain company growth and scale up, we need simple, effective models that *everyone* can follow—not just you or me. And we need consistency across the board."

"Oh, well." The employee shifted in his chair. "I guess—I guess that makes sense. It's just that sometimes new models and whatnot complicate things. I don't like complicating things."

"That's fair. Every new model takes time to get used to. I'm with you. Let's lean into the new model over the next two or three weeks. Can you commit to that?"

"Yes. Yes, I think so."

I waited a few moments to see if that was the end of it. It wasn't.

"I just have this issue at home," he said, kicking off a

fifteen-minute conversation about family, responsibility, and work-life balance.

Did that employee leave my office a perfect top performer? No. Utopia is a terrible destination. But if you show your victims, naysayers, and bystanders you care about them, they'll care about you, too. Even one crucial conversation can transform them into a better person, leaving you with a better culture—and a better organization—as a result.

It took me a while to understand that people bring their lives with them to work. They bring bills, debt, divorce, a child's poor grades, sick parents, and the list goes on. Just because they are sitting at work doesn't mean their heart and brains are there too.

Those conversations are twenty minutes well spent.

We all have blind spots because we are human. We are not humans who think with emotions. We are emotional human beings who think. When we can pull out our thoughts and get them on paper or in someone else's ears, we can begin to discern whether we need to address them.

Think of it this way: "Your truth" is what you tell yourself. It is the image you have of yourself and the desire you have for what others see. "The truth" is what they really see, hear, and feel. Just knowing the difference is truth, and the truth will set you free.

Reflection: Let's Go Inside

1. Do you know your blind spots? What are they?
2. Who would you ask?
3. Will you ask? When?
4. Are you afraid of the truth?
5. Can you make time in your life for LOVE?

6. Learn—What are you learning about, reading, listening to, and experiencing?
7. Observe—What do you know about the people closest to you? Family, friends, coworkers?
8. Vulnerable—When was the last time you made a mistake and were willing to admit it to others?
9. Encourage—When was the last time you encouraged someone who did not deserve it?
10. Who in your life needs encouragement? Will you give them encouragement? When will you give this to them?
11. Can you encourage yourself? Why? Why not?

PART II

Foundational Principles

CHAPTER 5

A Culture Committed to Change

Many moons ago, my grandma and grandpa watched all thirteen of us grandkids on rotating weekends. On hot summer afternoons, they drove us to Daisy's Diner in historic downtown Miamisburg. At Daisy's, my favorite meal was a beef hotshot—a roast beef sandwich with mashed potatoes in the middle and gravy all over. After lunch, they drove us to the toy store and bought each of us a new toy, like a model car or airplane. Then we went home with them and watched *The Lawrence Welk Show* and *Hee Haw*.

One weekend in early summer when I was eight years old, I woke up before the rest of my cousins. I saw my grandpa working on his lawn mower and asked him, "Can I try cutting your grass? Please?"

"I don't know, son."

"Please, Grandpa! I promise I'll do a good job. I promise I will!"

"Oh, all right. Here." He wheeled the lawn mower to the edge of the grass for me.

My grandpa's old-school push mower didn't have a blade guard. Step too close, and it would cut your feet off. If you could buy them today, you would find them right next to the yard darts!

His yard was the size of two conference rooms. The sidewalk leading to the front of his late-Victorian home split the grass into sections. Not too difficult a job for a youngster, right?

Off I went. I leaned my ribs up against the handle and pushed with the force of my whole body. By the time I'd gotten the first two rows mowed, my cousins had gotten up, eaten breakfast, and scampered down to the levee behind the house to hunt frogs. And where do you think I would have rather been? I quickly skimmed the front yard for the tallest grass and headed straight for those spots. And only those spots.

Done!

"Right," my grandpa said with an exasperated sigh after taking a look through the front window. "You didn't come here to cut my grass. You came here to play with your cousins. I'll finish it later. Just go."

He closed the garage door, and I stood watching him, thinking, *I told him I'd do it, and I didn't. I need to finish it.*

After he headed back inside, I wheeled the mower back out and picked up where I had left off. A job that should've taken twenty minutes took me over an hour. I wanted to be thorough. Grandpa watched me the whole time.

When I finished, he said, "Now, this is amazing. You did a really good job."

"Why did you let me quit the first time?"

"When you stopped the first time, this grass said, 'Scott did this job, and Scott doesn't care,'" my grandpa said. "My neighbors always compliment my lawn, and I didn't want to show them your name. I wanted to show them mine. I wanted to erase your name and put my name over the top because, Scott, whatever you touch, you put your name all over it. If you don't want to do something, don't even try. Don't touch it."

It was a harsh rebuke for an eight-year-old, but an excellent lesson for reforming an organization's culture. When I was a Destructive Hero, my name was all over the culture I'd created around Victoria and our sales team. And it was half-assed. But I committed to change. I didn't "mow" only the rough patches. I cut *all* the excess. If there's anything I can put my name on today, it's my passion for culture and the people it serves. Culture makes the world go round. But a bad one spins your entire world right off its axis.

CLOSING THE GAP

If you're going to close your culture gap, commit to change. Unless you do something intentional to change your employees' less-than-ideal answers about you and your company, they won't change. Closing any culture gap isn't easy. It takes courage. As leaders, we have to find the courage first and foremost to *not* be comfortable, especially in this post-recession economy. You can't have courage and be comfortable at the same time. Likewise, you can't be afraid of change while grateful for the opportunity to change.

As leaders, we should be afraid of leaving our culture the way it is. We should fear what our culture *could* look like if left unreformed.

Fear and gratitude cannot live inside your brain at the same time. Your desire for and commitment to a renewed culture comes from a sense of gratitude. Fear is about ego. Let gratitude win every time.

And along the way, it's OK to make mistakes as you close your culture gaps. Fail fast, fail forward. Focus on progress, not perfection. Only one thing is worse than a perfect person, and it is someone who *thinks* they're perfect. The march to perfection paralyzes everyone around you. Nobody wants to work for a perfectionist. Leaders who are interested in progress create followers, not fans. Unfortunately, many leaders run their organizations like they're in a track-and-field competition. They race around the track at full speed, lapping everyone else. So the others drop out, trudge up the bleachers, and just clap. "Look at him go! He's so fast!" they cheer.

Leaders in a high-performance culture—one where *everyone* enters the race—seek out the employee in last place. They put their arm over the person's shoulder and walk them across the finish line. Everyone watching gasps, "*Wow!* I will follow that person anywhere."

Care more about everyone finishing than showing off your talents. In the real world, this might look like the president or CEO relinquishing control over communication efforts inside the organization, from town hall meetings to official company correspondence like newsletters. I hate to break it to you, but you are not the smartest person in the room. If you are, I wish you all the best during asset liquidation.

Great leaders let everyone else speak first. Then the leader wraps it up, praising everyone. That's a posture of progress your employees will appreciate. You don't have to wait until the next meeting to close the gap. You can courageously, vulnerably, and progressively move to reform your culture *right now*. Remember your victims, naysayers, bystanders, and believers? Of course, you do. You're thinking about the last interaction you had with each of them right now. You need their honest-to-goodness opinion. You need to know, in their words, what they're seeing, feeling, hearing, tasting, and smelling in your culture. How else will you find and fill the gaps? If you could do it yourself, you wouldn't have bought this book.

• • •

THE FIVE SENSES OF YOUR CULTURE

Identifying the five senses of your organization's culture is simple—and downright terrifying. Hire an MBA student from a local college to interview at least three victims, naysayers, bystanders, and believers. In their interviews, expect your believers to offer to take a bullet for you. Expect your naysayers to chirp, moan, and bitch about your latest dumb idea. Good. Sometimes the worst of your workforce speaks the truth nobody wants to hear.

Schedule the interviews at a third-party location, but don't give the independent interviewer anyone's names. Your employees must feel insulated from even the hint of retaliation. Give your HR department the task of setting up each interview so you don't even know when they happen.

When your unbiased interviewer meets with your employees, have the interviewer say, "Your employer deeply cares about this organization, and they care about you. We want to identify the company culture gaps that they're not aware of, much less know how to correct. I'm going to record your answers, but not your name. Now I'd like you to close your eyes for a moment."

This brief sensory deprivation taps into people's emotions. Your interviewer then asks, "When you think about walking into the building, what do you see?"

An employee might describe physical objects like desks or computers, but they move pretty quickly to the intangible. "I see smiles," they might say. "But they're fake. I see pessimism. I see arrogance."

Your interviewer asks them to articulate their remaining four experiences: "What do you feel? What do you hear? What do you taste? What do you smell?"

"I feel purposeless, like I'm here to get a paycheck twice a month. Nothing more."

"I hear praise, and I know my boss means it. She's a good person."

"When I get paid, it tastes like crap. I'm leaving this buffet line the first chance I get."

"I smell motives, but I can't tell exactly what they are."

In your employees' answers, you'll find the truth. Maybe you've always told the press you have a loving and friendly culture, but your employees say they hate you. They're friendly to customers, sure, but they definitely don't like *you*. You can't paint *loving* on the wall of your office in good conscience, now can you? Nobody will believe it. Maybe *friendly* is all you've got. The secret is to simply be honest.

If, for example, your company sells VHS tapes and DVDs, you are not a creative, innovative, or disruptive company. I'm sorry. You're not. Maybe you were years ago, but not today. Never tell the world, much less your own people, you are what you are not. An organization's vision is a desired state, almost an impossible position of inspiration. But there is a difference between a dream and a delusion.

If you, as a leader, are willing to look at the truth, you can close any culture gap, no matter how wide or deep. Since you've approached the five senses of culture with questions, not commands, you've got answers you trust. Deploy those answers. Deploy them courageously and vulnerably, and give yourself time. It took years to create blind spots. It might take years to adjust them.

MAKING YOUR CULTURE LOOK RIGHT

You know what your employees want your culture to look like. Make it so. If the receptionist is always grouchy, it's time for her job description to include smiling. If the place is a dump, hire a janitorial crew to clean your building until every office is spotless. And if your values are real, publish them on the walls. But don't just tell. *Show.*

If you walk into McGohan Brabender, you'll see dozens of framed pictures of each employee's family on the wall. Our employees told me they value family, so that's exactly what they should see every single day. As their employer, we take away from family time five days a week. So, we turned the utility room into a toy closet. I want our employees' children to like the name "McGohan Brabender." When Mom or Dad says, "Hey, I have to go to the office and pick up a file," their kid says, "I wanna go, too! 'Cause I get to go to the toy closet!"

One of the greatest gifts anyone gives their children is a work-ethic role model—getting up for work every day on time. Then when we come home, we talk about work in a positive way. They see a work ethic they can emulate. But if we come home and bash the boss, kids put that in their pocket, and they become the next generation of victims, naysayers, and bystanders. I wouldn't wish that culture on anyone.

Let your building look inviting to newcomers, too. Any candidate or client who walks through McGohan Brabender's front doors sees a gigantic picture of a little girl wearing a giant space helmet, below the word *imagine.* You don't have to get that creative or buy foosball tables to make your work environment look different from your competitors' businesses. Don't let the place look like your dad's Oldsmobile. People should come in and think, *I want to know more about this place.*

Some employees will want to step into a role and make it their own. For example, our receptionist has been the receptionist for twelve years. I've told her she has earned the right to move anywhere she wants to inside the company, and I'll even pay for whatever training she needs. But she's happy where she is, and we are so grateful.

What if I hadn't asked? What if *you* don't ask? Your people may not see opportunities to grow. They may think the role they have is the role they'll always have. Never leave your people alone with their thoughts. Great leaders reach out to every employee and ask, "What do you see in your future here? What does the next stage of your career look like?" Then do whatever the hell you must to let them pursue their potential. If they're looking to move to a management position, tell them to lead their department until someone tells them not to. It's self-generated initiative. That's how your people earn promotions, new responsibilities, and a salary that makes everyone jealous. Then coworkers will ask the newest person promoted, "How'd you do it?" And they'll reply, "Lead until someone tells you not to."

The idea of nurturing your employees might scare you. But I promise, it's the best way to let your organization's racehorses run free and grow. And in turn, they'll grow your business. Give them a fence line and, if you can, grow an eye in the back of your head.

Most businesses also need plow horses. These are the hard workers who follow their job descriptions but rarely challenge the status quo. Then there are people with creative energy. They're thoroughbreds. You want a racehorse to go as fast as they can and win the race. But a racehorse needs a lane. Give them free rein, and they'll make messes all over the place.

If your thoroughbred employee is outgoing, let them win the business-development race. Send them out to meet people at events, conferences, and parties. Tell them their job is to meet as many people as they can and report back on who they met and how they're going to follow up.

Your introverted racehorses prefer a different sort of freedom. Let their imagination run wild. Tell them, "Imagine we started this company over tomorrow. Unpack for me what this organization could look like. I want to understand from *your* viewpoint what it should look like. What tools and resources would you need? What does the end state look like?"

Give them permission to think. Not everything they come up with will be workable, but any acceptable ideas they generate may be your company's next breakthrough. If you keep your thoroughbreds corralled in their cubicles, you'll never see their potential.

Job descriptions are the starting point, not the ending point. Does your organization allow creative, energetic people to run free, or do you hold them back? Never hire thoroughbreds to be plow horses. Unless you're the government, keep G1s and B4s and F2s out of your head. Titles that describe exactly what employees are permitted to do aren't fair to anyone. Provide clarity, yes, but nobody wants to put in 110 percent for an owner with control issues. Employees want to be led, not commanded and controlled. Give your people expectations to live up to.

I get it. Relinquishing control is the *last* thing you want to do. If you started your company, you started it with one desk—yours. Maybe you rented an office. You got a computer. You sold your first account, put that check in the bank, sold your second, and hired your first employee. Command and control are all you've ever known.

When I open my presentation "The Five Senses of Culture," I break the ice with a simple question: "Who here is worried about sitting here right now and being away from your company?"

At least half the room raises their hands.

"That's too bad," I say. "That means you don't have a business. You have a personality. A business runs when you aren't there. A personality has to be there for things to work."

If you're ready to finally start working *on* your business, not *in* your business, get clear on what your employees want to see. Do they want to see a personality whose ego keeps everyone toeing the line? Or do they want to see themselves fulfilled at your organization?

Consider what gets you out of bed in the morning. What do you think about when you wake up, get into your car, and head to the office? Your employees should see in their mind's eye a reason to get up and go to work. Do you know what inspires them? Do you know where they see themselves five and ten years from now? Ask them. Then tell them where *you* see them five and ten years from now.

"If I walked in here ten years from now, what would I see you doing?" you might ask your accountant. "Do you have an idea of where you'd like to go within the company?"

"Well, you know, I really like advertising. I like promoting things on social media, and I'm good at it."

"Really? You're an accountant."

"Yeah, but I studied marketing in college."

"Then maybe accounting isn't your lane here. If you see yourself in marketing, let's consider a plan to get you there."

Put people where they see themselves, and they'll thrive. And when your employees thrive, *you* thrive.

MAKING YOUR CULTURE FEEL RIGHT

You also know what your employees want your culture to feel like. Make it so. How a culture feels is a direct result of the company *vision* and *mission*. These are not to be confused with your *brand*.

Your vision is what you want to create in the world, and your mission is how you're going to get the good work done. I've always believed that vision without execution (a mission) is a hallucination. Yet execution without vision is a delusion.

Spend time asking people—your employees, customers, and truth tellers—for their ideas. If you have the courage, call a competitor that you admire. Tell them you are asking for their help. You will be amazed how much they will share with you.

I sit on a board of advisors for a company in Dayton, Ohio. A young man, Michael Whalen, wanted to buy a company and found one that was for sale. He bought it and quickly closed the doors. He called a competitor across the country. He told the owner that he admired his company and wanted to learn from him. This is the crazy question he asked the owner: Would you be willing hire me for free for ninety days?

Michael drove to the company, knocked on the front door, and told the owner he was ready to work. He spent ninety days inside of that company. He would drive to jobs with the owner. The other employees got resentful, but it was a good lesson for the employees. The owner told them if they showed that much interest, he would spend that much time with them.

Michael wanted to get dirt under his fingernails; he wanted to see and feel what success looked like. The owner told him everything in ninety days, and when he left, the owner wrote him a check for his time. Michael rejected the money, but the owner told him that Michael had given him so much more than he'd expected. Today, they are still great advisors to each other and dear friends.

A few months back, I met an HVAC entrepreneur at a leadership event about vision and culture. To kick off our chitchat, I asked him, "So, what do you do?"

"I sell heating and air."

"OK, that's . . . specific," I said. "When do customers buy heat and air?"

"They buy a new unit when the old one breaks or when they move into a new place. Simple."

I spotted a teachable moment. "How many other companies in the US can say they sell heating and air conditioning?" I asked. "Thousands, maybe tens of thousands?"

"Probably, yeah."

"Then what are your vision, mission, and brand? No, they are *not* all the same thing."

"I've got a vision to sell more AC units!" He chuckled. "My mission is about finding more customers and selling them units. And I guess my brand is, 'We're the company to call when you need a new AC unit.'"

"Maybe, but can you think differently about this? After all, your vision is *why* you do what you do. Does that make sense?" I asked. "Why do you do what you do? Why do you sell heat and air?"

He thought for a minute. "So people can have a comfortable atmosphere."

"*Yes!*" I gave him a high five. "You sell heating and AC units so people can live comfortably. If that's your *vision*, then your *mission* is *how* you do that."

"It's on demand." Now his eyes lit up. "My mission is to help people create comfortable atmospheres on demand."

"Now you're getting it," I said. "If your vision gives you your mission, and your mission drives your brand, what is your brand?"

Again, he thought for a minute. "Maybe my brand shouldn't be selling one-offs to customers. Nobody's getting any heat or air if that expensive unit they bought breaks down."

"What if, instead of selling units, you *leased* them? Technology is always changing anyway, right? Instead of irregular one-time sales, you build long-term profitable relationships. And every few years, customers get a free unit upgrade. Their heat and air improve, they're always comfortable, and you have recurring revenue your competitors don't. I'd say that's a win-win brand."

"I'd say so, too."

"That's a hell of a lot different from your competitors. It takes tremendous courage to say, 'I'm not going to sell AC units. I'm going to create comfort-on-demand environments.'"

"Yes, it does. Hang on a minute, Scott." He excused

himself, buried himself in the corner of the room, and wrote out his new business plan.

That's the power of aligning your **vision, mission,** and **brand**. You can't help but feel inspired.

Now, let me ask you, are *your* people inspired? Do they feel like everything they do contributes to a cause greater than themselves, greater even than the organization?

At McGohan Brabender, our **vision** is **to empower healthier living**. We do this by empowering businesses with solutions so they can create jobs, keep jobs, and grow their companies. We empower people with choices so they can make better decisions, which drives better behavior, which drives better health. I don't know about you, but *that* vision feels a lot more exciting than "We sell health insurance."

When we bring a new customer into the building, we want them feeling that energy. We want our workforce thinking, *You know what? We can impact that organization. We can impact our community. We can make a difference. It's not just more work. It's a new opportunity.*

Make sure your people understand your vision. Too many leaders talk about *what* they do, not *why* they do it. (Pick up any book by Simon Sinek, read it, and soak it in. It will change your life and your company.) Talk about your why—your vision—every single day, and you'll change the landscape of your organization. It's hard work. Do it anyway.

When a workforce understands their why, their ability to follow your company's mission is off the hook. Your mission is *how* you carry out your vision. For example, at McGohan Brabender, our **mission** is **to provoke people to think differently, reveal new opportunities, encourage action, and provide a path**. This flows directly into our **brand—good, smart people effectively managing the entire healthcare dollar**.

I'd like to say I came up with these vision, mission, and

brand statements on my own. I didn't. We had employees willing to tell the truth when asked. I'd also like to say the first
drafts read so eloquently. They didn't. In the original version of
the vision statement, four paragraphs of word salad followed
the words "Empowering healthier living . . ."

When I announced this new vision in the company news-
letter, someone took me aside.

"Hey, that's good. I'm not sure I can remember all that, but
I see this word 'empowering,' and then 'healthier' down here,
and then 'living.' Why don't you just say, 'Empower healthier
living'?"

That makes too much sense. We need more words, I thought.
Thankfully, my ego agreed with the revised version.

To make these statements stick, we produced a short
video. It's usually not a story for outsiders; it's a story for us at
McGohan Brabender to remember who we are. See if you can
spot the spirit of our three statements appearing in the script:

> In our world, change isn't optional. It's neces-
> sary. Where there's change, there's a challenge.
> Challenge accepted. We are agile advisors
> forging new paths in an involving marketplace.
> Our mission? To change the way you approach
> health benefits. Here's the thing: when you've
> got healthy people, you've got happy people.
> Trust us, we know. We are our own test sub-
> jects. We live our programs day in and day
> out. So when we say our methods are tried and
> true, we mean it. We've got the insight to cut
> through the chaos surrounding health bene-
> fits, and we share that knowledge every chance
> we get because we believe that the more you
> know, the more equipped you'll be to make
> smart decisions.

We take your health personally, literally. From the groundbreaking solutions we develop to the customized service we give. It's hard work, but we wouldn't have it any other way. Because taking care of people is in our DNA. Besides, we've all got a little something to remind us why we do what we do. And at the end of the day, when all is said and done, we can celebrate knowing that we don't just make more birthdays possible, we make healthier birthdays possible. McGohan Brabender: empowering business, empowering people, empowering healthier living.

Reinforcing vision and mission didn't end here. My board of advisors at Aileron held me accountable for reminding everyone what we do, how we do it, and why.

"Every week for the next eighteen months, write a blog post for your workforce telling them what your vision, mission, and brand statements mean. You're not allowed to go off target."

By the time I was tired of writing and talking about it, I heard people around the office say, "I think this is clicking. I think I'm getting this."

Today, nearly all people inside the company can recite all three statements by heart.

MAKING YOUR CULTURE SOUND RIGHT

Once you get feedback from your workforce, you'll also know what they want your culture to sound like. Make it so.

A manufacturing CEO hired a consultant to interview his company's victims, naysayers, bystanders, and believers, as I'd suggested. When I asked him how it had gone, there wasn't a way for him to tactfully share people's feedback. One of my core values is not to use offensive language, but this answer deserves brevity and honesty. He said, "All I heard was, 'You're an asshole.'"

That's honest . . .

Apparently, employees hated the *Keep off the Grass* signs that guarded the company headquarters' acres of gorgeous green hills. In context, the message meant for customers was "We care about our image!"—but employees *heard* their CEO telling them, "I care more about my grass than about you sorry people."

The next day, the CEO called hundreds of employees to an emergency meeting.

"I'm sorry. You're allowed on the grass now," he said. "In fact, we're going out there right now. I'm going to tear down those signs, and you will stomp all over that grass. You're more important to me and to this company than any treated lawn."

This simple gesture turned an upside-down culture right-side up. Telling your employees what they need to hear repairs relationships and restores trust. In your company, you may not have to get so drastic as to hold a special meeting to apologize. Your people may need to hear from you, their leader, more often.

Admitting our mistakes is important; accepting them is where the beauty of change occurs.

Every once in a while at McGohan Brabender, I meet with employees and give them a safe space to talk about what's going on in their jobs without their direct reports present. We talk about what has happened in the company, what went well, and where we can get better. When your employees hear their own voices, they realize they have a voice. That's powerful.

◆ ◆ ◆

MAKING YOUR CULTURE TASTE RIGHT

You also know what your employees want your culture to taste like. Make it so.

When you see employees tasting success, turn them into heroes. Write about these people. Talk about these people. At McGohan Brabender, we celebrate our culture heroes on our Raving Fans Wall. When a customer sends a note of appreciation, we read it in front of the entire company, put it on every TV screen, and have the employee sign the wall in permanent ink. When you see people living up to your company values, prop them up on the nearest pedestal. Let your high-energy, creative people taste validation. Do that for them, and they'll do the little things for you.

When a caravan of clients arrives for an on-site McGohan Brabender training in the pouring rain, an army of umbrella-carrying employees meets them at the curb. Nobody asks them. They do it. I'm telling you; you can't buy that.

We also celebrate each employee. When it's someone's birthday, we write handwritten birthday cards—one to every single employee—and we put a fifty-dollar gift card in each one. We don't buy those prewritten cards; we get the blank ones. We take the time to write a paragraph. We want more employees hearing, "You matter. You're part of a story. You do great things around here." Stick a gift card in there, mail it to their home, and you've got yourself followers, not fans.

When tragedy strikes inside or outside your organization, let your people taste empathy. It breaks my heart to remember the 2016 Great Smoky Mountains wildfires. Arson claimed the lives of a McGohan Brabender employee's daughter-in-law and both of his granddaughters. After search-and-rescue teams fought for days to locate them without success, I watched our culture—our family—wrap their arms of love around him. When the devastation of a cancer diagnosis struck one of our employees, I watched their coworkers show up to work with shaved heads. When your employees taste the empathy of their coworkers (including you), that's when you know you have a real culture of love.

These stories are all around your organization. If your door is shut and you are too close to the business and not close to your workforce, you will miss them. Go look for them and ask people around you to collect them. You don't need to spend money to start making a difference. Telling a beautiful story is free, and everyone loves stories. The most powerful element of a story is that everybody wants to be a story or part of a story. Tell a story, and it gives people permission to jump into a new chapter and create their story for your organization, for you, and most importantly, for them.

MAKING YOUR CULTURE SMELL RIGHT

You also know what your employees want your culture to smell like. Make it so. Employees are a bit like children—they see everything, whether you want them to or not. They also smell everything. The question is, what do they smell? Do they smell genuine motives or a hidden agenda? What do they smell when you announce your new culture initiative?

Your motive to close the culture gap should inspire everyone around you. What sort of organization do you aspire to be in the future? Don't borrow someone else's slogan or message. Don't try to be Apple, Google, or Starbucks if you're not. Deliver your own message, one that sounds like it comes out of your mouth and your heart. Even the interns can smell fake inspiration, so don't be fake. Be authentic, and you'll find everyone around you following suit. If an employee's mom passes away and you say, "I know what you're going through," and your mom is still alive, people smell your agenda a mile away.

Don't sacrifice authenticity for the appearance of empathy, or you'll lose both.

When the five senses of culture function well inside of your organization, things get easy. They get fun. If more leaders took the initiative to repair their culture like you're doing by reading this book, maybe more than 13 percent of people would enjoy their jobs.[2] Then, maybe we could set the world back on its axis.

Reflection: Let's Go Inside

(If you do only one exercise in this book, please do this one.)

I suggest you try this exercise in two formats: one for yourself and one for your organization.

Go back in time and write down the best place you have ever visited. Write down what you saw, what you touched, what you tasted, what you smelled, and how that place made you feel.

What about you? Close your eyes and explain to someone what it was like to be with you. Go back and remember dating someone. You had questions, and you asked people about this person. Imagine bringing yourself home to meet your parents. What would you say about yourself? You talk too much, you are shy, you are too serious, your jokes can be offensive, you are sweet or kind?

Imagine, if you will . . . you are introducing your best friend to yourself. What would you say?

Be careful here. They say in life that the truth will set you free; it does not have to sound good, it just has to be honest.

For example: I want to introduce you to Scott McGohan. He has a lot of energy and is passionate about life. He tries to be humble but gets distracted quickly. He can't say no and commits to too much. He is more interested in how you feel versus what you think. He is not afraid to be vulnerable, but in his core, he is sensitive to criticism. He is kind, his faith matters, and his family is more important today than ever.

1. What you will see: Image is more important to him than he is willing to admit, so he will be put together and enjoys being the center of attention. (His wife likes to call him a show pony.)
2. What you will hear: Mostly words of compassion, vision, faith, and vulnerability. He has improved his listening skills but can interrupt and take over a conversation.
3. What you will touch: He is a hugger. He is more sensitive to the world today, and he will be careful, but if you are an introvert, you might be overwhelmed.
4. What you will smell: Hopefully someone who is authentic, but like most human beings, he will be deciding whether you can make his life better or worse.
5. What you will feel: You could be overwhelmed; he won't care. He hopes you leave the interaction better than you showed up, and he will love you no matter what.

So . . . your turn . . .
What would people see?
What would people hear?
What would people touch?
What would people smell?
What would people feel?
What did you learn about yourself?

CHAPTER 6

Culture with a Cause

Famous investor Warren Buffett said, "It takes twenty years to build a reputation and five minutes to ruin it." The same can be said of culture. I've seen it too many times. The C-suite member, president, or owner pushes a fancy new culture initiative, the workforce buys in, and morale skyrockets. But before the new company values freshly painted on the conference room wall dry, everything is back to "normal." The same squabbling among coworkers. The same "silo" behavior. And the same hypocrisy. It can take years to build a culture and five minutes to ruin it.

A reformed Destructive Hero lives life with a cause. They think beyond what *they* want and consider a purpose that includes *others*.

WHAT SMELLS IN HERE?

By this point in the book, you've invested time—even resources—learning and implementing a new way to build your culture. The last thing either of us wants is for your workforce to forget the vision, mission, and brand that *they* helped write.

Unfortunately, this happens more often than you might think. Culture maintenance problems trace back to the same one of the five senses of culture every time—smell. Now, you might be thinking, *Wait a minute, Scott, we covered the smell! I've got it!* "Culture maintenance" means cleaning out every garbage can. Otherwise, the smell of that forgotten rotting banana peel will overpower all the other positive smells you worked so hard to set around your culture like scented candles in the office. Nothing spoils a fresh culture faster than the stench of hidden agendas. What's worse is that you don't even have to *be guilty* of an ulterior motive. If employees don't outright smell an agenda, a certain number will be skeptical enough to imagine one. Then they'll spread their ideas around, and everyone will think something is up.

Why are they changing things now? Why all of a sudden does my opinion matter? Why did it never matter before?

They must be up to something. Is he/she retiring? Are they planning on selling the business?

What the heck is really going on around here?

It's the funniest thing, isn't it? You go through all this trouble reforming your culture only to make employees suspicious. If you haven't heard rumors about an impending retirement or sale yet, you better believe you will soon. Once your culture initiative is underway, you've got to be intentional and thoughtful about how you prove to your workforce that this culture—your new way of doing business—is going to stick. If your employees don't believe your new attitude is sustainable, good luck sustaining a positive outlook yourself!

Every leader wants a high-performance organization in which a good work ethic is the norm, not the exception, and where employees represent you well to your customers. You need employees to *trust* that this new push is authentic. That it's legitimate. That it has them in mind. This culture thing is not you trying to stroke your ego or build up a strong company valuation.

One effective way to gain (and keep) employees' trust over the long haul and build a sustainable culture is to let them see you get behind something that has no profit motive. Something that demonstrates that your new culture is all about making the world a better place. Everything you've done up to this point to diagnose culture problems and reform them has only been training. Now you're ready for your first real test. Your first battle. You're going to rally your people together and embody your company's values.

A MOTIVE FOR GIVING BACK

Show your people you're serious about this culture thing. Show them you're serious about living up to your values and being a role model for the entire organization. Align with a cause that allows you to show that a real change of heart has occurred—and your new culture is not the result of ulterior motives. Get honest with them regarding where you were, where you are, and why giving back is important now. Be vulnerable about why you were blind to this before and what you are trying to accomplish. This is where the rubber meets the road.

This is where you get to see if you're everything you say you are. You can't turn a cause over to somebody. You can't delegate altruism. Giving back is essential. Your community has given you so many assets already, from your workforce to your customer base.

There is a difference between a personal cause and a company cause. Try not to confuse them. If it is your passion but doesn't align with your organization's vision, that's OK, just try not to embed it in your organization as a cause.

The first step in choosing a cause you can support is to make a list of organizations that might be close to your own vision, mission, and brand. Invite employees to be part of your cause-selection process. If you've identified a word or feeling you want your workforce to get behind, call a meeting or put out a memo and ask them what causes they can think of to support that word.

Take compassion, for example. If your workforce is in their forties and fifties, they might have parents dealing with Alzheimer's, a terrible disease. Your company cause could be volunteering at a senior center. Maybe your people are passionate about alleviating poverty, homelessness, and other socioeconomic burdens. Choose a local nonprofit that helps get people back on their feet. And you can't go wrong with dogs and cats! Donate time at the local animal shelter. If you need inspiration, call city hall. Say, "Our organization is looking for volunteer opportunities for a day. Do you have suggestions for us?" I guarantee you they will throw more ideas your way than you'll ever need.

Once you poll your employees and compile your list, ask your workforce to vote on their top two or three causes that are most closely related to the work they do every day. Encourage your people to whittle the list down to a single charity that everyone can get behind. At McGohan Brabender, we've got a Giving Back Committee that looks at different charitable organizations to see which ones fit best with our business.

Our founder and my dad, Pat McGohan, taught us to give back to a community that gives to you! In our MB Gives Back program, every employee gets one day to give back. Every employee in the company gets eight hours to volunteer at any charity in the community. We don't care who it is, where it is, or how you do it. Lead with your heart and lend a hand to what matters to you.

To give employees volunteering opportunity recommendations, the Giving Back Committee looks for charities that are well-run, have low administrative fees, and devote 100 percent of donations to charitable work. That's why we chose Shoes 4 the Shoeless. They serve schools with a high percentage of students in a subsidized lunch program. Most of the kids in these school systems either wear their brothers' and sisters' shoes that are too big or their own shoes that have grown too small. Shoes 4 the Shoeless gives free shoes to an entire school system. What's great about that experience is every volunteer gives students individual attention. They have a conversation with the students. They have to get down and put shoes on their feet. It's an act of humility, an act of compassion. Just a brand-new pair of shoes can make a child smile. We've brought twenty or so McGohan Brabender employees to volunteer at Shoes 4 the Shoeless seven times. I always feel like *we* get a heck of a lot more out of it than the students do!

I bet you 90 percent of the other people in that room who aren't McGohan Brabender employees don't know who the shareholders are. We are not walking in there like we are the owners, and neither should you. Walk in with your company, with your coworkers. And every once in a while, when someone asks, "What are you guys all about?" maybe an employee will say, "Oh, that's one of the owners over there. He (or she) will tell you."

STUMPING FOR A CAUSE

Why is this cause important to *you*? Why is this cause important to the organization? And why is this cause important to your employees? You'll need to write your stump speech— your elevator speech for your cause.

When you talk about your cause with employees, make it clear that it's not about you. The cause is your cause, but it should be bigger than you. I can't tell you what your cause should be because it must be yours. What I can tell you is that people will rise to something bigger than themselves, bigger than *you*, if it feels real and authentic. Memorize your stump speech and repeat it without reading it. And no pauses or "ums." No hesitation. Share it from your heart to your people, for your people. Don't show up like it's a concert and you're the rock star. Show up with humility, learn, and experience each other outside of the office.

Your speech should be less than a paragraph, and you should be able to deliver it in front of your workforce at the drop of a hat. It should resonate from your heart and sound like your own words. And you'll want to go through your company one by one and tell everyone why the cause they've chosen matters.

Let me say this again: *Do not lie about your cause.* If my motive is profitability, I'm going to be honest. "Hey, we're trying to get them as a customer, so that's why we're volunteering there." But if you're motivated by compassion, be intentional about reminding employees why you're doing what you're doing.

When you arrive at a volunteer event, set an example for everyone else. Be the first one there. Work the hardest and the longest. Be the busiest person in the room. It's an incredible team-building experience. It allows your team to see you in a completely different light. Employees need to think, *I've never seen our CEO like that before.*

Your cause also shows you what your people are all about. You get to listen and watch them. You pick up clues about their interests. You get to see their work ethic in a new environment. You'll also get to see who's on their phone all the time and who's not into it. You'll see employees you *thought* were the most extroverted get quiet because they're in foreign territory. You'll also see the normally quiet ones smile and come alive in the new environment. Then reward yourself and your people by going out to lunch, feeling warm and fuzzy, and talking about the experience.

"What are we encouraged by? What are we *discouraged* by? What did we learn about ourselves? What did we learn about our *business*?"

Ask strategic questions to carry this team-building experience back into the office, and you won't just be piling into a car and throwing soup into bowls. What you *don't* want is your workforce patronizing society. If they're going along with it to suck up to the boss, there's no point. You want them to give back and be humble in an honest way. If you or your people are doing all of this out of ego, other people are going to smell it. So, take on a cause you care about, and your people will know that this new culture—the one that makes them look forward to Monday mornings—is here to stay.

You're getting more than ROI: return on investment. You're getting ROP: *return on passion*. And that's an asset you won't find on any balance sheet.

Reflection: Let's Go Inside

1. What organization means a lot to you? Why do you lean into this organization?
2. Is there a cause your organization leans into? Why do you think they care so much about this?
3. How can you incorporate your passion into an organizational purpose?

4. Would you be allowed, encouraged, or discour-
    aged to transfer this into your organization? If so,
    by whom, or are you simply afraid? Get honest
    about what is holding you back today.

5. Would you be willing to try until someone tells
    you not too? Why? Why not?

CHAPTER 7

Culture Heroes

A reformed Destructive Hero can be a culture hero. The bottom of the pit can be a beautiful place as long as you know you are there. When you're at the bottom, you have three choices—dig, sit, or climb. Most choose to sit or dig. But the ones who climb never want to return to the pit.

When my daughter, Courtney, turned sixteen, I bought her a new car with a big red bow on top. But when my son, Taylor, turned sixteen, I had to sit down with him and explain why I couldn't buy him a new car, too.

"I'm ashamed to admit this, son, but your dad is a sick dude. I'm getting better. My understanding of love has grown so much in the past few years. I used to just give stuff, not time. Financially, I can afford to buy you the car you want. But emotionally, I can't do it."

I loved his response.

"Well, Dad . . . part of me wants my old dad back so I can have that brand-new car. But another part of me likes the new you a lot better than the old. So, I understand."

Taylor is now twenty-seven years old. He owns his own company and is more financially disciplined than I ever was.

I learned, he learned, and today, he is a hero of hard work, financial discipline, truth, and kindness in his culture. I'm glad I dug myself out of the hole so my son didn't have to.

CATCH THE CULTURE BUG

Whether it's family or business, culture reformation starts at the top, but it cannot end there. For example, if your business's reference point is customers first, you, alone, can't create a customer service experience that sets the industry standard. That's up to your employees. It's impossible for you to foster a culture day in and day out after you've cast the vision. After all, you have a business to run! You can't be with every customer and every client. You can't be on every page, at every visit, on every phone call. Not unless you're a business of one (in which case, you don't have a business; you have a personality).

Sole proprietors do have complete control of their culture. If you're not a sole proprietor, your business needs culture heroes. Culture heroes keep a values-based company culture alive. They "infect" everyone in your organization with the culture bug, whether you have five employees or five hundred. And any time an employee is "inoculated" against the values your company lives by, your culture heroes run them out of your building without the hassle of management intervention or human resources drama.

At McGohan Brabender, we've hired people who didn't work out the way we had hoped. We *thought* they were a good fit. They weren't. They put their heads down, shrugged off our values, and did the minimum work required. Most of the time, MB's culture heroes wore them out or showed them a way to leave. Culture heroes live and breathe culture, and they can spot those who don't. And when they do, they call them out. I can't even imagine how much paperwork, how many resources, or how many headaches our culture heroes have saved us. Actually, I can. *A lot.*

One of our middle managers approached his assistant after lunch one day. "Hey, I expensed my lunch at McDonald's today," he told her. "If anyone asks, we had lunch together. Got it?"

His assistant—a culture hero—came straight to me.

"I'm really uncomfortable with this," she said, holding back tears. "Integrity is one of our values. I don't know what to do."

"You did the right thing. We always try to do the right thing for everyone," I said. "I'll handle this."

I was afraid to deal with this. But as a reformed Destructive Hero, I learned that when I am afraid, I should move. *What you tolerate, you encourage.*

I walked over to the offender's office.

"Hey, I saw this lunch on your expense report," I said. "Who did you have lunch with?"

"My assistant."

"Great."

I spoke with HR, then went back to the manager.

"Today's your last day," I said as I shut the door behind me. "You asked another employee to breach our culture. You made her uncomfortable. If you're willing to compromise our culture just to cheat us out of six dollars, you have no place here."

"You're going to fire me over six dollars?"

"No. It's so much bigger than six dollars, and I hope one day you figure out why. All the best."

THE FOUR CS

If you're going to shoulder the burden of reforming your culture, it only makes sense to put in the effort to maintain it.

But who has what it takes to be a culture hero? How do you find your culture heroes? As a leader, it's your job to identify the character traits you expect of your culture heroes. That's where the Four Cs will help you. I've found the ideal culture hero traits are **character, chemistry, competence**, and **collaboration**.

I don't make it a point to physically call out who is a culture hero and who is not. It is not a title that goes beyond my perception. Labeling can be destructive if the guidelines are not clear and defined. My intent is to have a pool of people to go to if I want the culture to shift. Here's why this is important.

We all have poor performers doing good things. They are making progress, and that is positive. The real issue here is when you call that out publicly or personally. If someone who is a low performer does a great thing, and the other people around you know they are a low performer, you calling that out in public becomes confusing to others.

Bringing this to light is such a delicate balance. If you don't understand these issues, you can create subcultures and give low performers some power they haven't earned.

Let me explain what **character** means to me. People who have character keep their promises, regardless of the cost. Whether that promise is getting back with a customer or meeting your father for dinner, keeping your word reflects on your character. Anyone I trust as a culture hero must have a strong character.

Our character is often learned from our parents or people around us. We can develop good character, bad character, or a mix of both. We might have developed bad character traits out of fear or to protect ourselves. Excessive anger is a good example of poor character (the intensity of which is normally based on protecting ourselves versus our real feelings toward the person or issue). By intensifying our good character, we develop ourselves. Your character inside and outside of your company is all you have.

Chemistry means your culture heroes or champions have positive employee relationships. When I review comments from a customer about a wonderful experience, I want to hear positive feedback. "This person motivates me. We connect so well. I trust this person." If someone has chemistry with their coworkers, chances are high they're a culture hero. Chemistry is rooted in self-respect, self-awareness, and mutual respect for others.

Competence is more than the ability to complete a task. It's learning the fundamentals of your business and passing on that wisdom to coworkers and customers. Competent people go outside their job description and relentlessly pursue professional learning opportunities, such as skills training and advanced subject matter expertise. Your employees have a responsibility to grow themselves inside and outside of your business. With the right people, you can serve your customers well. Effort is important, but increasing skill is even more important. Your current path of training and people development must evolve. That doesn't mean everyone has to be alike. We're all different by design, which is the gift of humanity. But your employees' ability to adapt, learn, ask good questions, and most importantly, listen increases their ability to navigate customer and coworker situations. Competence is a must-have in your culture heroes.

And lastly, **collaboration** is just what it sounds like. It's all about teamwork. And it encompasses all the other Cs. Collaboration includes **character** (What's your motive?), **competence** (Do you know your stuff?), and **chemistry** (Do you inspire others?). If all of these are apparent in your culture heroes, then their ability to collaborate increases. Collaboration is the secret ingredient to doing everything well. Collaborators build consensus. Collaborators ask questions no one else has the foresight or courage to ask—then they work with their teams to find answers. They're direct, not implicit. They're prescriptive, not reactionary. If you ask a collaborator to call a prospect before 5:00 p.m., they'll do whatever it takes to get ahold of that person before the close of business. If they're the employee giving the request, they'll explain themselves. "We need to get ahold of this prospect before 5:00 p.m. because they're leaving for a two-week vacation tomorrow." They don't assume you know things that you don't.

One more message to keep in mind: culture heroes must represent the company in all of its facets. I can't have a bunch of fifty-year-old white males as my culture heroes. If your workforce is diverse by gender, race, and age, your culture heroes must be, too. Make sure your heroes represent the workforce and look like the people you see in the break room every day.

Keep these ideal culture hero traits in mind during your recruiting, interviewing, and hiring process. At McGohan Brabender, we used to bring candidates in to meet with four different hiring managers one-on-one. It was uncanny: every interviewer had a different opinion of the candidate!

Instead of the candidate doing four individual interviews with the hiring managers, now the candidate sits down with the four hiring managers at the same time. The questions we ask line up with the Four Cs. But you don't have to stop there. If you take time to articulate what traits matter to *your* culture and why, they might be different than the Four Cs. And that's OK! The big question is *why* are these traits so important to your business?

When you define the traits you want your culture heroes to possess, don't look for perfection. Look for consistency. Your culture heroes don't just believe in your mission and vision, they *embody* them. Here are interview questions that have served us well at McGohan Brabender:

"We believe in making promises you can keep. How are you intentional about getting back with people? What's your process for being responsive?"

"We're all different on this planet. All of us have different personality traits. Inside your existing organization, is there somebody different from you in regard to how they carry themselves, how they act, and how they behave? How do you collaborate with them?"

"In what ways are you a continuous learner? What are you reading? What information keeps you up to date in regard to your industry and your strategy?"

"Explain for me an area or an issue inside your organization where you and a team member had a collision on an initiative. How did you work through that together?"

CALLING ON YOUR HEROES

Now that you know what to look for in your culture heroes, the next step is calling them out. Business is always about people. Always has been, always will be. Good, smart people will always pick recognition over compensation. So will your culture heroes. These men and women of your inner circle won't expect a higher salary to foster your culture. They'll volunteer when given the opportunity.

Walk the hallways of your office. Acknowledge those who already have ideal culture hero traits, whether they know it or not. Ask to speak with them in private and say, "I've identified some qualities that are important to me as a leader, and you're an example of them every day. I need people like you to keep this company alive for the future. I'm not going to be here forever, but this company's values will. You're a torch carrier. You're a leader. You challenge your coworkers to live up to our values, and I wanted to let you know it hasn't gone unnoticed. Thank you for being part of us."

You could formalize the process if you're willing to do the hard work and *empower* your culture heroes. Give them a voice and put resources behind it. Meet monthly and listen to your team of heroes. Be willing to give your culture heroes permission to go out and test their new ideas. Then let *them* go out and execute. Don't be tempted to micromanage. Focus on how you can support the execution. Then ask them to come back to you with a progress report. How is the organization better or worse? How did the idea work or not work? Rinse and repeat.

Show your culture heroes you take their role seriously. Allocate funds for a culture budget. It doesn't have to be huge. Think about holidays, birthdays, and other special events that might come up. Your heroes will love the opportunity to bring some happiness to their coworkers, and the extra effort will put a lot of smiles on your employees' faces.

Work with your culture heroes to ensure that your culture budget reflects the core values you want to reinforce. To remind McGohan Brabender employees how much we care about family, we put our money where our mouths are. We give every expecting mom an extra four weeks of vacation. The spouse gets two weeks' extra paid vacation. This policy leaves out adoptive parents, so our culture heroes came up with a legal-fee reimbursement policy for mothers and fathers who can't have biological children—adopt a child into your family, and we support you up to $5,000. On top of that, we deposit $2,500 in all parents' flexible spending accounts every year to help with daycare costs. Since the employer takes parents away from their kids, it only makes sense to help with childcare costs while the parents are at work. My father told me something I've never forgotten. "Scott, if you want to do something amazing for a person, do something for their children." He was right.

DON'T LET YOUR CULTURE
BECOME A CRIME SCENE

Nothing builds culture faster than the right investment. Your appointed culture heroes are in the best position to help you determine which ideas will provide the best return. For this same reason, beware the *self*-appointed culture heroes. Self-appointed culture heroes mean well but execute terribly. Without your official invitation, meetings, and two-way accountability, your culture goes awry. I know because self-appointed heroes left their mark on the walls of McGohan Brabender several years ago.

After an internal meeting addressing long-term profitability, a group of employees decided that their coworkers were abusing company-purchased office supplies. New BIC pen and Post-it note deliveries several times a month add up. I later learned they repurposed a janitor's cart to patrol the hallway, office, and cubicle to collect unused office supplies from their coworkers' desks. Several times, the after-hours task force rummaged through the "crime scene" at every desk to find out how many extra legal pads and unused paper clips employees had collected.

Epic disaster. Morale plummeted. Employees rebelled. Thank goodness our true culture heroes called these people out before it was too late. When we found out about the office-supplies police, we killed their initiative immediately. We met with the entire workforce, explaining that we, too, make mistakes. It would have been shallow to blame only the offenders since an internal meeting had lit their flame. So, we owned it, put a stop to it, and then cleaned up the mess.

Our employees are like elephants. They have long-term memories. Mention that stupid cart to a McGohan Brabender employee today, and they'll remember the time they thought about quitting. All because a few people wanted a black-and-white culture where everyone had to watch their backs. They infected our workforce with their own culture virus, and the ensuing plague almost wiped out our whole team's motivation.

After our employees recovered, we empowered our true culture heroes and the workforce with a clear example of our culture. Over the next six months, we set out to tell specific stories about our culture, our employees, our customers, and what it means to be on the McGohan Brabender team. Some were about specific team members and the goals they had helped accomplish. Some were about interactions with customers and the problems we had solved for them. Some were hilarious, others profound. Every few weeks, a story would go out as a memo to all employees.

People love stories. Create stories about your culture, and tell them over and over until people own them. Remember, a culture belongs to the people who work in it. But do they *know* it belongs to them? And do they carry it? If you're not sure, go back to your reference point: your customers. They'll tell you. All you have to do is listen.

Reflection: Let's Go Inside

1. What does **character** mean to you? What is it? What is it not?

2. What does **chemistry** mean to you? What is it? What is it not?
3. What does **competence** mean to you? What is it? What is it not?
4. What does **collaboration** mean to you? What is it? What is it not?
5. Do you have a culture hero? Who is it?
6. Can you wear the cape? Why? Why not?

CHAPTER 8

A Culture of Cooperation

I've always disliked being picked for a team. Golf, Ultimate Frisbee, dodgeball. Why does this still bother me so much? As a kid, I was not a good athlete. Sure, I could play backyard sports, but if the game got complicated or stressful, I wasn't much help. Word got around the playground quick. So, when other kids picked teams, I was never first. I just hoped I wouldn't get picked last.

About ten years ago, I was with a group of high school students for a day of paintball. (Yes, even guys in their early forties like to play paintball! I know, I know. Don't judge!) After everyone suited up, the two most athletic kids picked their closest friends for their teams. It was like pulling teeth to get them to pick the misfits like me who were left.

"Tell you what. Let's stop the picking and choosing," I said. "You all"—I looked at the huddle of kids nobody wanted on their team—"come with me. Instead of two teams, we'll have three teams."

The two team captains looked relieved.

Off to battle we went. On the way, we bumped into the guy who ran the paintball field. I had an idea.

"Real quick, can you give my group some tips on how to win?"

He looked us over as if to say, *Wow, good luck.*

"Stay on this field. Right here. Everyone else will be moving from field to field. Don't shoot or move until they come toward you. You'll hear the other teams approaching. If you stay hidden and listen, you'll get them every time."

My group was the smallest and the clumsiest by far. But with those simple instructions, we *won.* We didn't have the same skills the others did, so nobody would've bet on us. That's OK—we bet on ourselves. We cooperated, believed in each other, and treated each other like equals.

I took away a powerful lesson from that paintball event— how you treat *anyone* in your organization is how you treat *everyone.* It is easy to care about the rock stars, the best of the best. But I grew up as an underdog, and people gave me a chance when they didn't have to. People love underdogs—go love the underdogs!

We must be careful not to surround ourselves with people who look like us, sound like us, and work like us. An organization is a moving, living, breathing organism. When we have a healthy respect for the differences in people, we begin to accept who we are and who they are.

I watched my father do this so well over the years. He would treat everyone the same and had an uncanny ability to move past the people who might have had titles and authority to visit the people who didn't. Today, I hear many leaders inside McGohan Brabender say, "We have to try to do what was natural to Pat McGohan and make it intentional in our lives."

That's a powerful legacy to leave any organization.

Whenever McGohan Brabender onboards college freshmen and sophomores as interns, we don't give them busywork nobody else wants to do. We treat them like apprentices whose job it is to support our people in doing their best work while learning the same work ethic that our employees display. And we, in turn, learn from our interns. Thirty days into our summer internship program, we ask every intern the same two questions: "How do you feel about the work you've been doing here? Do you have any advice for the company?"

I hear the same response over and over again: "I don't feel like I'm at the bottom of the totem pole like at other jobs I've had. I feel like what I do here matters, like I'm adding value to the company. I'm never looked down on. Keep doing what you're doing."

I take Jesus's words about serving "the least of these" seriously. When your employees feel like their value as people is not based on their value as *employees*, they feel like they belong. Whether you're a summer intern or in the C-suite, you know your work matters—not just to your department, but to the entire company.

Good cultures get into trouble when silos form inside the organization as a result of day-to-day operations. If you're not careful, every department becomes a clique, an in-group with its own sense of belonging. Once you let these silos form, natural competitive drive makes them hard to break. Finance, marketing, and sales elect unofficial team captains, and employees feel like they're back in grade school waiting to get picked for the baseball team. Sure, some will have a sense of belonging, but everyone will know where they stack up. Someone always gets picked last. How do you keep these silos from forming? How do you make sure you don't end up dealing with cliques and popularity contests?

CUSTOMER CULTURE JOURNEY MAPPING

Of course, you want a single culture inside your company— not competing cultures. You can often see this inside an organization when sales gets all of the applause and the rest of the people accept it and work just to get by.

I saw this play out one day in a meeting with an owner of a large transportation company. He asked if anyone had questions. Many hands went up. The owner looked at a person in the front whose hand was up and asked the person a terrible question. He said, "Are you revenue or overhead?" I thought to myself, *Did he really say that out loud? Is he calling truck drivers revenue and all others overhead expenses?* The person responded that they worked in billing. He said, "That's overhead. I will take questions from the revenue side of the organization first." He asked the revenue people, truck drivers, if they had any questions. Oh, they did. When he asked if overhead had any questions, you can guess they had none.

I am confident he had a good heart and wanted a good company. But he was completely blind to the power of words and the value of a culture that appreciates every single piece of the organization.

When people feel like they belong, they cooperate and work better together. Fostering cooperation (rather than competition) starts with breaking open those silos. At McGohan Brabender, we walk all our employees through a customer journey exercise to communicate the value of every person working together. Here's how to do it.

Think about a transaction from the very beginning. Say a prospect or a customer calls your business. Your marketing department made that call happen. And when that first call comes in, your phone system must have the capacity to manage the incoming and outgoing phone calls. You also need somebody who *answers* the phone. Your receptionist is led by somebody who has told them how to behave, how to operate, how to work inside the organization, and what the company culture means. Your prospect needs to hear a smile through that phone call. Then that call gets transferred to a salesperson or an account manager. From there, this pending transaction touches everyone else inside the organization, from finance to human resources to payroll.

Just thinking about your prospect's journey into and through every part of your organization won't eliminate conflict or competition between departments. Every person needs to see with their own eyes how interdependent their job description is with everyone else's. Actually walk through what happens when that phone rings. Buy a spool of yarn and gather your workforce together. Hand the spool to marketing first, who will pass the spool to the receptionist. Then the spool goes to quoting, shipping, receiving, accounting, finance, invoicing, and whoever else aids in completing the sale. When you're done with the exercise, the yarn should look like a spiderweb.

Holy cow! your employees will think. *I really am part of something bigger.*

Every transaction touches every person inside your organization, from the front door all the way to the back door. Relentlessly honor everyone involved, rinse, and repeat. Why honor? Because all too often in the typical workforce, people think, *Sales are the only ones who get any credit around here. They're the only ones we cheer for. What about me?*

To create that sense of belonging, make sure you're honoring and recognizing every person in the organization and where they fit in that spiderweb of a transaction.

At McGohan Brabender, we're on a quest for success stories all the time. And when we find them, we celebrate them together. Remember the Raving Fans Wall? When a client sends a note to anyone in the organization, we read that thank-you note or email testimonial in front of the entire workforce. Then they sign their name on the Raving Fans Wall. Some people have signed the wall over and over. We're intentional about making sure it's not just sales getting all the praise. We're acknowledging every part of our business.

But when the same people continue to receive thank-you letters every month, other employees think, *I want to get a thank-you letter. What do I have to do to get noticed by a customer?* So have your heroes tell stories about what they did for the customers who reached out and thanked them. It takes a lot of work to handwrite and mail a letter. Even sending an email requires valuable time. Nobody can mandate that a customer sends a thank-you note. Your employees have to earn the right to receive one, and having employees who have received letters explain how they earned them will motivate others to do so.

Through this or a similar process, you'll make sure everyone knows their part and is honored for the role they play. But as every leader knows, teamwork for teamwork's sake isn't good enough. You want *productive* cooperation. You want your people working together happily so the company remains sustainable.

A SPIDERWEB IS FULL OF STRAIGHT LINES

The key to keeping your employees happy *and* allowing them to do their best work is process improvement. The straighter you can make that yarn, the faster and more efficient (and profitable) every transaction will be. Even inside of a great culture, people can spend their days doing what *feels* good, not what *does* good. They tend to create busywork for themselves on slow days, which makes everything complicated and clunks up your business model. Then when they do get busy, they have that busywork *plus* their actual work.

But don't try to tell your employees how to do their jobs better. Ask them to take ownership of improving their own processes. Start right after the Culture Journey Mapping exercise. It should go a little like this:

"We're going to make our best attempt at turning this yarn into one straight line. There's a good chance that inside your department, you know a lot more about your role and your process than I do. Help us straighten out this line for speed and efficiency. What are the activities you do for a customer? List them all."

When our employees did this exercise, we identified 385 total activities we performed from the front door to the back door for every transaction. Then we looked at all those activities and asked, "Which ones would a customer *pay* us for? Which would they willingly write out a check for and say, 'This is awesome'?"

We send birthday cards to all our customers. Now, I doubt a customer is going to pay us to send them a birthday card. Maybe they wouldn't pay us to do that, but birthday cards amplify our culture and illustrate that we care about people. So that's going to stay.

But then we found other activities we were performing that had no redeeming cultural value, and no one was going to pay for them. I don't know how they even ended up in the sandbox! It was like some cat had dropped this activity in here. Time to scoop it out!

One example was our customer-relationship management software (CRM) accuracy. When a client called in with a question about their employee health benefits, what happened if all the details weren't put into the CRM? The employee then had to get up from their chair, find a physical file, validate the details, and return to the phone call. Because so many employees did this every day, we found an easy way to straighten the yarn. When a client first joins McGohan Brabender, account managers now log all the accurate client details in the CRM. No more searching for them down the road.

I'm sure you have similar activities taking up space inside your organization. Don't micromanage your employees and reprimand them for wasting time. Empower them to identify and solve the problem themselves, then honor them for a job well done.

"QUIT DOING MY JOB!"

Another problem many organizations struggle with is employees doing other people's jobs. In our customer service department, we have MB Advocates whose job is to fight on behalf of our clients. But we discovered that our long-time salespeople tried to fix client problems themselves without enlisting the MB Advocates. Some of these folks had been with McGohan Brabender for years, and they feared that if they passed client problems off to another department, they wouldn't be handled in a timely fashion. While I appreciated how important our culture and our clients were to them, it wasn't an efficient way to do business. The team has their own responsibilities, so this role switching slowed down sales momentum considerably.

We straightened that yarn by setting up an inbound call system. All customer service–related calls now get a support ticket. And all of those tickets can be tracked and rerouted back to our MB Advocates team. With this system in place, our salespeople can see who's working on what at any time, they know the clients are being taken care of, and we can confirm that nobody is doing someone else's work. That gave the MB Advocates enormous confidence to do their jobs. Our salespeople got to stop doing extra work.

We wouldn't have discovered this problem (or the solution) without the yarn spool exercise. Our sales team was making the most noise about taking care of clients while MB Advocates were making the least. I grew up in sales, and salespeople are great at making noise. The issue is to discover what is "their truth" versus "the truth." There is always a big gap here. Don't try to make it perfect. Just try to understand it at a deeper level.

Leaders often get stuck listening to the loudest noise, and they start there first. But usually, your quiet department is the most effective. So, when you identify problems in your customer journey after the yarn spool exercise, go to your least-noisy people, the ones who work hard but never complain, and tell them, "Look, you're an amazing part of our business. We don't hear any negative feedback in regard to what you're doing. Another part of our business is having some issues, and we need your help. What assets can you bring out of your department to help this other department perform better?"

SINGING THE UNSUNG

Praising the quiet ones at McGohan Brabender takes me back to our values as an organization. Culture values aren't words—they're a way of doing business. For McGohan Brabender, family means taking care of our people, and taking care of our people means clean work environments, places where people feel like it's taken care of, it's safe, and it's a great place to show up to work.

We have four offices: Dayton, Cincinnati, Columbus, and Indianapolis. I recently met with the building owners in Columbus regarding their cleaning crew that was in charge of cleaning our office. They were downright terrible! The place never looked clean. They would leave their supplies sitting out on the windowsills. There was always debris on the office floor. Our receptionist bought a vacuum so she could make sure the floors stayed clean!

I told the building owners, "This is intolerable. Our agreement clearly states that your crew will clean our office. You're harming our values, and you're nicking our brand. We're putting in our own time and expense to do your job. I don't want to threaten consequences for your sloppiness, but we've had this conversation over and over again. Either we leave, or you reduce our rent as compensation. Or better than that, I will give you time to come back to us with a solution that fits our values, not yours."

When I left the meeting, I realized that I had never heard a whisper about the people who clean our Dayton building. The same husband-and-wife team—Paul and Sharon—have cleaned that office for ten years, and it's been immaculate every morning. They broke a coffee mug on my desk once, and they glued the handle back on, wrote me a note apologizing, and bought me a new mug the next day!

Paul and Sharon help us live up to our values, and I hadn't taken proper notice of them until now. We sent out a company email, asking our people to take a moment and write them a quick note thanking them for their hard work. We had one hundred people write them thank-you notes after sending out that one email. That night when they came in and cleaned our building, they knew we felt grateful for who they are and what they do, and as a result, they're going to take care of us. Our employees didn't have to take the time to write notes, but once we saw a problem elsewhere, we realized this location of our business was always clean. For a decade, we never saw them nor appreciated them. We neglected to see the value of what they brought to our business until evidence of problems elsewhere made us appreciate them.

CAN YOU SEE THE PROBLEM AND IGNORE THE NOISE?

Look at your organizational chart and the boxes for every position. Let's start with your shipping manager. Don't think about their name yet. First, ask yourself, "What does my business need from a shipping manager?"

Then look at the employee. Is your current shipping manager valuable to your organization? Are they looking to the future to help your business? Or are they only somewhat valuable but self-centered and noisy? If so, there's a good chance your new shipping manager is the person who reports to your current one. And your employees will work better together once they're in the right roles. Go back to your chart and see if there's a better position to which you could pivot your current shipping manager. If not, it may be time to say goodbye.

Look at your chart again. Your noisy people are often the naysayers, the bystanders, or the victims. Maybe they're tired or burned out, and maybe you have given them too much credit for the noise they've created so far. Instead of making changes based on their noise, call their bluff. Take a strong effort to be honest and try to motivate them. If that doesn't work, this might not be the place for them anymore.

On the opposite end, your future-oriented employees, when out of control, can be somewhat dangerous. They can be like thoroughbreds who want to run free with their ideas. They can be exhausting and overwhelming, but I'll take them over the naysayers any day. I would much rather have to put reins on somebody and hold them back than have to tie a rope to them and drag them along.

If you do need to let someone go (and they haven't done anything downright destructive, like steal from you), be open and honest with them. Do this, and they may go willingly. Be sure you're open and honest with the rest of your team, too. Let everyone know that the person has been let go and offer to answer any questions about it one-on-one. The last thing you want is a bunch of rumors about why someone was let go or to leave your employees wondering, "Who's next?" Avoid blame. Focus on the need for change.

At the end of the day, everyone who belongs at your company will value teamwork as much as you do. And they'll want to work with others who value it, too.

Reflection: Let's Go Inside

1. Do you have silos in your organization? Where are they? Why do they exist?
2. Can you tear them down? Why not?
3. Do you have silos in your life? Why?
4. Have you mapped out the process from the front door to the back door and understand every "belly button" the process touches?
5. What do you see that can change?
6. Are you willing to address the current process? What would happen if you did? What would happen if you didn't?
7. Who is the noisiest person in your organization? Why do you think they make the most noise?
8. Who makes the least amount of noise?
9. Are there unsung heroes in your organization? Do they have a voice?
10. Can you give them a voice?

PART III

Building for the Future

CHAPTER 9

A Workforce-Attracting Culture

When I was a Destructive Hero, I only cared about myself. I *thought* I cared about others more than myself. Honestly! I was so delusional.

Relationships don't have to be hard. Attracting and retaining the right kind of workforce is all about storytelling. Sounds strange, doesn't it? Your job as a leader is to collect amazing stories about your staff and their accomplishments, then broadcast them online where future (and current) hires can see them.

My wife and I went to a New Year's Eve party with a bunch of friends. Often, when my wife and I go to events together, she doesn't know many of the people, so leaving her alone while I make the rounds is rude. (Even so, as a Destructive Hero, I did it often.) But these were friends, and we both knew most of the people there.

It was late when we got into the car to head home. While I drove, she talked about the evening. She went on and on about one person and then another and another. She told me stories about whose lives were tough right now and who had it easy. She told me what their kids were up to and where they went on vacation. Then she asked me a question I didn't have an answer for.

"So, how was your evening?"

Great, until now. I didn't have the courage to tell her I had not one thing to say about anybody. I'd been so busy talking about myself that I hadn't asked even one person a question. I didn't give anyone the chance to talk. I bounced from one person to another, bragging about my accomplishments. You see, I wanted to be seen. My wife wanted to connect. She invested her time in people because she was interested. I invested in myself because I was arrogant. But where did that arrogance get me? That drive home felt so lonely.

I still think about that night. Now when we go to events, we spend most of the time together. I make sure I ask every person I talk to a question about their lives. In return, I get to experience genuine human connection. My only regret is that I didn't stop talking and start listening sooner. And it's not just something I practice at parties. No matter how big McGohan Brabender grows, I'll always call every employee by their name. After all, you can't build a culture if you can't surrender *self.*

THE MOST IMPORTANT WORD

Do you know the two most important words in the English language? The first one changes depending on who you are. Care to guess what it is?

Your first name.

If you're in a big crowd and someone yells a name, you probably won't turn around. But if someone in that same crowd calls your name, you immediately look.

The second word never changes. That's why I consider it the more important of the two, making it *the* most important word in the English language.

It is "help."

Get great at asking for help.

Go back to that big crowd. If someone yells "Help!" you turn around and look. It doesn't matter who you are or who shouted it. The urge to help is universal.

Asking for help is one of the best-kept secrets to building a culture that attracts and retains high performers. *Everybody* wants to help. *Everybody* wants to feel useful. Why? Because what goes around comes around, and *everybody* wants to be helped when they're the one in need. Therefore, the leader— and the organization—that asks both "Can you help us?" and "How can we help you?" has a distinct advantage in the hiring and retention marketplace.

It's common sense. Think about it. Most leaders tell their employees, "I'm the boss. I get to say what happens around here. And I say you're not doing enough. We're not perform- ing well enough because of *you.*" You separate yourself from every employer in your industry when you say, "We're under- performing as an organization, and no one person or depart- ment is to blame. But we can get back on track if we all work together. Can you help us do that?"

Remember the yarn exercise?

Give your people the opportunity to rise to the occasion, and they will. I'm not saying you have to. As long as you're not breaking any laws or running afoul of regulations, capitalism allows you to do whatever you want. That's one of the benefits of America. Still, I hope your goals go way beyond your profit margin. In uncertain economic times, leaders who want to succeed don't have the luxury of behaving exclusively accord- ing to the profit motive.

$$\bullet \quad \bullet \quad \bullet$$

ATTRACTING (AND KEEPING) TOP PERFORMERS

But, Scott, I don't want to do that, you might be thinking. *I'm the only one taking the risk.* Fair enough. But know that this attitude causes two problems. First, you're going to have a hard time keeping your existing workforce unless you adopt a different mentality. And second, you're going to have a hard time attracting a new workforce. When candidates become new hires, show them a path to grow inside your organization. In this economy, you're not only fighting to retain your workforce, but you're also fighting to attract the younger, tech-savvy, purpose-driven generation as well. Why make your life harder than it needs to be?

If your workforce doesn't get to experience the authentic you, you leave people to their own imagination, which isn't a good thing. **Sometimes, your brain is like a bad neighborhood—you shouldn't be there alone.**

Can I trust the boss? (I am not a big fan of this word, by the way.)

Can I trust my coworkers?

Can I trust myself?

Don't let your employees get lost in that bad neighborhood. We all can get lost in our heads, and when we do, we beat ourselves up.

I'm not good enough . . . I'm not smart enough . . . I'm not thin enough . . . I'm not pretty enough . . . I'm not handsome enough . . . I can't do this . . . I shouldn't do this . . . They'll laugh at me if I do this.

It's relentless, self-deprecating talk. Don't leave people alone with that, whether it's about themselves or about you. Our imaginations make things out to be worse than they are. And if your office door is closed and they can't see you, people will think you've got your feet on the desk or a putter in your hands or are making a list of the next cuts. Open the blinds! In our office, we knocked out an entire wall and pulled the blinds out of floor-to-ceiling windows so everyone can see what the CEO and president are up to at all times.

After all, your job as a leader is to work on the business, not in the business. Working on the business means removing barriers between you and your workforce. Get out there among the people. Be in a relationship with them. Be attentive. Be visible. If you're present, your people will match your effort.

THE THIRD MOST IMPORTANT WORD: THANKS

One important way to attract *and* retain your workforce is with gratitude. I may sound like a broken record, but I cannot stress how important it is to show your people—and the world—how thankful you are for all the work they do in your business.

If you're grateful for your people, how do you tell them that? How do you express it? Simple. You can write thank-you notes like we did with Paul and Sharon. You can leave them a voice mail or leave a Post-it note on their desk, but simply doing nothing is a terrible option. Feeling gratitude isn't enough. As leaders, we need to make our intentions come alive. We *want* to thank an employee for a job well done. But for some strange reason, our intentions often fail to land on that individual.

Handing compliments to people is a great thing. A lot of us, your employees included, are bad at accepting those compliments. Someone thanks us, and we say, "Oh, that's not a big deal. Don't worry about it. It's part of my job."

If I handed you a gift, you would unwrap that gift and be grateful and appreciative. A compliment is like a gift. It took time for the person to think about what they would say, just like shopping for a gift. They spent time wrapping it, similar to the words they used to tell you how much you mean to them.

We should be able to receive compliments the way we receive a gift. But so often, we don't accept their gift. We use sarcasm, we shrug it off—the equivalent of throwing their gift on the ground or returning it to the store. I was the worst at this. I grew up with low self-worth. I had teachers who told me I was worth it when I didn't believe in myself. They told me I *was* good enough, smart enough, and athletic enough. I was telling myself, *I suck. I'm stupid. I'm not athletic.* People from the outside world told me things about myself I could never see. Your employees are no different. A little genuine praise goes a long way.

TRY TO BE SPECIFIC

Build momentum around telling your people why they're worth it. If you're having trouble figuring out what to say, turn the question around. From a leader's perspective, what words of affirmation mean the most to you? Instead of getting caught up thinking about what other people need to hear, think about affirmations that others have said to you. Ones that have meant a lot to you. It's as simple as that.

For people at McGohan Brabender or community members who don't mind cameras, I sit down in their office or cubicle and interview them for a Thankful Thursday, a social media exercise I've done every Thursday for two years. I say to the person, "Hey, you know what? I'm super thankful for you and the difference you make, and I'd like to shoot a short video and just talk about you as a person. I don't have any interview questions, and I'm not going to talk about work. Let's just talk about you."

People want to be part of a story. Invite them into your organization's story by spending time with them. Understand them. Often, as a leader, it's tempting to micromanage your employees and attempt to take on their roles. But that's not constructive for building a relationship with them. After all, it's their sandbox, not yours. Resist the urge to get up in people's faces and say, "Why are you doing it that way? That's not the way we used to do it. You need my help with that." Never forget that your organization has grown beyond you.

For shy employees or more introverted ones who don't like being on camera, take them out to lunch—just you and them. One-on-one. You can put an introvert in front of a crowd, and your attempt to lift them up can tear them down. Understanding what motivates people is important.

Caring about these personal details is one of the fastest ways to show your employees you care—or don't. If you go to lunch with an employee and ask, "How are the kids?" and they say, "Well, I have one," or "I don't have kids," then you've shown them you're following a set of generic questions and you don't know anything about them. But mention their wife by name, their baby by name, and they'll know you care.

My advice to leaders is to tell people they're valuable to you and your organization and be specific as to exactly why. Make sure the reason is sustainable and repeatable. Words matter. Words like "you're terrific" or "that was amazing" don't tell the person exactly what they did so they can try to do it again. Someone once gave me great advice that was simple. I like things simple, and this was simple because it related to my favorite way to remember things, the rule of three. The advice was: SAR. The S stands for the situation. Describe the situation minus any interpretation or opinion. The A is the action that occurred, and the R is the result or the outcome. What behavior resulted in the action and created this result?

It's not that complicated. Maybe it is a personal, handwritten note to leave on their desk. Or those notes could be sent to their homes. It could be sending one email to one colleague once a week. It doesn't have to be an iPhone in front of your face talking about the individual on social media.

A HELPING HAND FROM THE TOP

Just as you want your employees to help your organization grow, you also want them to know you're there to help them, too. For example, I once read the story of a janitorial services company owner who asked her workforce how she could help them. Because she stayed in a relationship with them—and didn't try to micromanage by taking on their roles—they trusted her. And they told her.

"We can't get to work on time."

It turned out many of them had unreliable cars, shared a car with their spouse, or didn't have a car at all and took the bus. Unreliable transportation is a big problem when you're trying to hold down a good job to support your family.

Rather than blaming her employees, she helped them. She bought company buses. Now, every day, she drives around and picks up employees so they can get to work on time. That changed employee morale overnight. Pick up the book *The Dream Manager* by Matthew Kelly. It's a real gift.

In Chicago, a restaurant chain had to deal with a similar transportation burden on their workforce. During a product promotion fair, a beer distributor gave away branded koozie cups, shirts, and hats to the waiters and waitresses. One of the beer distributor employees came right out and asked a waitress, "Hey, how do we get you excited about our products? What would motivate you to shine for your customers?"

And the waitress answered, "Honestly, I'm having trouble paying for my transportation back and forth to work. I'd be able to perform a lot better if I wasn't constantly worrying about how I was getting home."

The beer distributor employee took this information back to her manager, and the beer distributor bought train and bus passes for every single employee at every restaurant location. An authentic leader finds out about the burdens on their workforce and does their best to alleviate them. Is it transportation? Compensation? Housing? You help them, and they'll show up for you and your customers in ways you can't even imagine.

Of course, you also want your employees to have a positive experience while they're at work. No use investing in employee transportation if they hate coming to the office! Consider sending a confidential employee survey to find out what your workforce wants to improve while they're at work.

This survey will be different from the five-senses-of-culture interviews. The purpose of those in-depth interviews is to hear from your victims, naysayers, and bystanders where your culture needs repair. The anonymous survey is for *all* employees. In the appendix, you'll find a copy of the survey we give to each employee at McGohan Brabender.

Reflection: Let's Go Inside

1. How many names can you list inside your organization or department off the top of your head?
2. Can you ask for help today? If so, why and from whom? If not, why and whom are you afraid of?
3. When was the last time someone thanked you? How did that make you feel? Have you ever told them how it made you feel?

4. When was the last time you thanked someone else? Who was it? Why did you thank them?

5. Have you ever been a part of an employee survey? Were you honest? If so, why? If not, why?

6. Have you ever conducted an employee survey? What did you discover?

7. What did you change, and why?

8. What did you ignore, and why?

9. Imagine if you will . . . if you could change one thing inside of your organization, what would it be, and why?

CHAPTER 10

A Culture for Everyone

One warm Sunday afternoon when I was a teenager, my dad took me and my brother to Community Golf Club, a local public course in Dayton, to play nine holes. We pulled into the parking lot ten minutes before our tee time. As my dad turned into a parking space, another driver was trying to do the same. The man jumped out of his car, ran up to our driver's-side window, yelled at my dad, and spit in his face. Yep, you read that right. The window was rolled down, and the man literally spit in my dad's face.

My brother and I tensed, ready to watch the fight of all fights come to blows right in front of us. That didn't happen. Dad rolled up his window, put the car in reverse, backed out of the spot, and held out his hand for the man to take it.

Dad found another spot, parked the car, wiped a towel across his face, and said, "Come on, boys, let's go play golf."

That was it. No words. No fists. No shame. I could tell he felt sorry for a person who, for some reason, had acted out like a child throwing a tantrum. Treating people right has nothing to do with others and everything to do with you. It was a great lesson for young Scott to watch.

I never saw my dad discriminate against anyone for any reason—not because of behavior, status, race, gender, or anything else. He had an uncanny ability to find and talk to the loneliest person in the room everywhere we went. I'm not sure where it came from, but passing it on to me is the greatest gift he ever gave me. We need to connect with all people of all backgrounds in our organization. You know where I'm going with this.

It's true—I'm a middle-aged, blond-haired, blue-eyed white guy. And I care about diversity. Why? Because I don't know what it's like to be African American, or Asian, Hispanic, Indian, or Middle Eastern. I don't know what it's like to be female or nonbinary. And I don't know what it's like to have socioeconomic struggles. But I *do* have compassion for all people regardless of age, race, gender, orientation, or economic status.

I watched this happen to me in an amazing way on a trip to Howard University in Washington, DC. We took two high school students on a trip through an organization that is important to me. We spent the entire day walking through Washington, DC.

A terrific young lady had a college orientation appointment at Howard University. She asked me if I would like to join her. I was honored, and off we went. I sat in an orientation meeting with thirty people—moms, dads, and potential students. I was the only white male in the room. My dear friend was with me and leaned over to me and asked an honest question, a real question without a motive. "Scott, do you feel out of place here?" My answer was yes. Then he said something to me I will never forget. He said, "Scott, it happens to me every day."

I thought I understood why diversity was important to me. I didn't. Today, I accept that I don't have the answers, but I *do* have the authority to find them and the passion to make it better.

To embrace diversity in your workforce, first take a look at your hiring process. Start reviewing résumés without looking at names or addresses. This small adjustment removes assumptions based on gender, ethnicity, nationality, and zip code. So many experts have talent in this area. The most important element is to realize that you can't do this alone. I can't, and I do not have the expertise, experience, or talent to move this needle alone. You are going to need help. Give yourself time.

Second, work backward from hiring to recruiting. At McGohan Brabender, 75 percent of our new hires come through referrals from existing employees. That's no surprise, given that a recent company poll showed that 90 percent of our workforce would refer family and friends.

Great people hang out with other great people. Schmucks hang out with schmucks. So, if you have great people from diverse backgrounds in your organization, say to those employees, "I think the world of you. We're looking for great people. My gut says you've got family and friends who are great people. Who do you know in your circle of friends that might be interested in working here?"

Without diversity, you leave people alone in their thoughts again. *Why aren't there more people like me here? I wish I saw more people like me. Maybe I'd fit in better at a different company.*

FILLING YOUR BUILDING WITH GOOD, SMART (DIVERSE) PEOPLE

Our economy and our communities are changing. In Dayton, Ohio, we have good, smart people from all over the world. I want to reach out and find those people. I grew up with a dad who I never saw discriminate against anyone— except people who were lazy and disrespectful. He treated everyone the same. I'm sure he never looked at a female employee and thought, *I'm going to treat her differently because she's female.* He had unconscious competence about people regardless of gender, race, or economic status. Often in life, we do what we see and not what we are asked to do. I am blessed to have watched him with his gift of simply loving people.

He cared about people as individuals, not as representatives of a group or a population. That's why I don't want a ranking system to check how many of this race, this ethnicity, or this gender we have. What I want to do is fill my building full of great people who happen to be diverse.

But if all we're hiring is fifty-year-old white guys, then dollars to doughnuts, they hang out with more fifty-year-old white guys. And that's who you'll keep getting. Then you'll be stuck going around in a circle because you'll make everyone who's *not* a fifty-year-old white guy feel like they don't belong. Break the circle and ask for help. Be willing to admit you can't change it alone, but people with expertise can. If you have the power to make it happen, go do so.

Do you understand which regions of the world are represented by people moving into your community? Do you understand the impact of the different issues females and males struggle with? What about your older employees or those with different sexual orientations? Do you understand the shifting demographics of your city?

Same isn't change. If we all look the same, we might just get the same.

We have different generations inside of our workplace walls. Understanding and working on interactions across generations allows for a more hopeful future. You need young, smart, energetic people in your workforce alongside more seasoned employees. And these young, smart, energetic people want to have families. Work is not the only part of their life.

Let them live out their dreams and aspirations, whether it is having a family, doing more charity work, or going to school. Do this, and you'll have a diverse workforce committed to your company—not just a compliant workforce. Compliant employees are a pain in the neck. They smile in your presence and sabotage you behind your back!

DON'T PICK ON GENERATIONS;
YOU ARE A PART OF ONE

Age is an important part of our identity. The generation in which we grew up drives our thinking. Realities are associated with age in the workplace. The terms *matures, baby boomers, Generation X,* and *Generation Y* have gained currency and carry with them many generalizations to explore. Most recently, the term I cannot stand is *millennials.* Ask them if they like the word. No, they don't. In fact, you'll get a "Hell, no." People picked on my generation, and people are picking on millennials now. They're people. We're all people. Why do we have to label them? Maybe we should just seek to understand each other.

When I grew up, people told me I would never be like the generation behind me. That was a lie, and I almost bought into it. Have you heard the phrase, "Give people a reputation to live up to"? We should give every generation the encouragement to make their lives and the lives in front and behind them better and stronger.

Too often, we act as if only the old are wise and only the young are curious and energized. Such stereotypes become lodged in our brains. By realizing this, we can assure the difficult issues of *all* ages in the workplace are recognized. Then we can apply all the creative ideas we can muster to be *one* creative team, across all ages, to drive *change.*

US Generations in the Workplace[3]

Matures, born pre-1944	2 percent
Baby boomers, born 1946–1963	29 percent
Generation X, born 1964–1976	34 percent
Millennials/Generation Y, born 1977–1999	34 percent

Matures' Formative Events and Values[4]

Events	Resulting Values	Perceived Liabilities
The Great Depression	Duty, sacrifice	Status quo
Pearl Harbor	Conformity, unity	Reluctant
World War II	Age = seniority	Avoids conflict
The New Deal	Hard work	Prosperity

Baby Boomers' Formative Events and Values[5]

Events	Resulting Values	Perceived Liabilities
GI Bill	Conformity (keeping	Process before results
Flight to suburbs	up with the Joneses)	Sensitive to feedback
The civil rights	Fear of technology	Avoids conflict
movement	Workaholic	
John F. Kennedy	Good at relationships	
The Vietnam War	Teamwork	

Generation X's Formative Events and Values[6]

Events	Resulting Values	Perceived Liabilities
The Cold War	Institutions will fail	Impatient
1970s oil crisis	you	People skills
Challenger explosion	Lack of heroes	Inexperienced
Computers	Techno literate	Cynical
Divorce rates	Thinking globally	Authority
	Creative	

Millennials/Generation Y's Formative Events and Values[7]

Events	Resulting Values	Perceived Liabilities
The internet boom	Family as friends	Attention
Technology	Optimism	Impatient
Terrorist attacks	Embrace diversity	Difficult people
Child-focused	Activist	Spoiled

When you look at this, you might see yourself spanning two different generations. For example, I am on the cusp of the baby boomers and Generation X. I was not alive for many of the events in the baby boomers' era. Some people who might have been born before 1945 only remember what is listed under the baby boomers' events. You fit where the events hit your heart. Either way, we can all relate to the idea of understanding each other.

The first time I saw this, it opened my eyes to what is around me. I grew up with three television stations, playing outdoors, and an overwhelming fear of Russian nuclear destruction. My first computer was an Atari with 16 kilobytes of memory (green screen, no color). We had no cell phones. Mom and Dad had to come outside and yell at the top of their lungs for us to come home. I could go on and on, but the point is simple: things change. I adapted to what we have now, but I have fond memories of how I grew up. The same is true for organizations like McGohan Brabender.

I cannot pretend everyone will have my values, my past, my dreams, and my experiences. If I do, I will lose touch with where we are today and what other generations bring to me, and I won't grow. That's what we are trying to do—*grow*. We will grow faster and better if we all participate. Every generation possesses assets and liabilities that we need to recognize.

Our past is responsible for so much of who we are. I look at my generation and acknowledge the assets that have driven me to where I am today. This has opened my mind and heart to where generations behind and ahead can help me. Their perspectives are different, and we can be grateful for each of them.

What can you do to make your organization friendly to diverse ages? Take millennials (whoops, I said it) and Generation Z. They care about student loan repayment. They worry more about tuition debt than 401(k) funding. Direct your human resources or people operations team to repurpose your employer 401(k) contribution to help your younger employees pay off their student loans.

WHO'S COMFORTABLE?

Think about what else you can do to make your company attractive to people with different backgrounds. Ask your current employees what they'd like to see you do differently. And ask the people you interview what they're looking for in an ideal company and an ideal job.

Have compassion for your workforce, and diversity can occur naturally. You won't have to fill checkboxes and seek out people of specific races, ages, orientations, or genders. After all, that's not true diversity. Diversity is love and understanding. In most cases, we bob and weave through life where we are comfortable. The real beauty comes out when we work through being uncomfortable. Just maybe in *our* discomfort we make others *more* comfortable. It takes hard work, and you will make mistakes. You're making some of them now, and that's OK. Seek to understand diversity and respond to that understanding with kindness and love.

If you make everyone feel welcome, people of all backgrounds will want to join your company, your home away from home. You'll build a true family of coworkers, all with compassion for each other and your customers. So maybe the exercise is simply shifting your point of view. Instead of looking at the mirror, we can try looking out the windshield and get a better view of what is happening around us.

◆ ◆ ◆

Reflection: Let's Go Inside

1. What does diversity mean to you?
2. What does diversity mean to society?
3. Did you grow up in a diverse community?
4. Who taught you positive traits about diversity?
5. Who taught you or spoke to you negatively about diversity?
6. What generation did you grow up under?
7. What did you grow up afraid of?
8. How has technology changed during your lifetime?
9. What is your opinion of the generation behind you and in front of you?
10. How could you interact more strongly with the generation in front of you?
11. How could you interact more strongly with the generation behind you?
12. Does it bother you when people speak about millennials? Why?
13. Growing up, did people "pick" on your generation?

CHAPTER 11

A Culture of Stop, Keep, and Start

When we recently decided to read our Glassdoor reviews, truth flooded to the top. The good news? The reviews all mentioned how everyone was approachable and authentic. But employees also brought up, over and over, concerns around what they called "middle management." Outside of the C-suite, leadership is different. That's a big concern. Frankly, middle managers in any company are the C-suites of tomorrow. No one's going to be around forever. Where does that mean this company is headed?

I'm not a big fan of feedback. I would like to *say* I am. I respect it and need it. I prefer *situational leadership*—actually addressing issues inside of the situation—instead of waiting for an annual review. Give people feedback, and if it's negative, they get upset. They go right to fight or flight. Or worse, they freeze. They disagree with you, quit within days, or scurry back to their office and never put in an effort again. Situational leadership gives you and them the freedom to have a different relationship.

It's a gift to speak with kindness and truth at the same time. Often, we use these independently. People can leave a conversation and have no idea what was said or, worse, what they should be doing differently. I have this curse and am working on this as we speak.

My normal place to start is to use kindness. In other words, I would tell you how great you were and then throw in a few areas where you need improvement. I would use my own interpretation of a situation and place my feelings inside of the feedback. That's not fair to you or me.

Here is the guide that helps me:

- **Keep doing** with kindness: Without interpretation and/or feeling, what was the situation I saw that I appreciated? What was the behavior I witnessed and the result?
- **Stop doing** with truth: Without interpretation and/or feeling, what was the situation I saw that I do not want repeated? What was the behavior I witnessed and the result?
- **Start doing** with hope: Without interpretation and/or feeling, what are the traits and/or talents the business needs to grow the person? What does this behavior look like to help them grow? What result does this effort bring forward?

If I was going to change my mindset to giving feedback, I would need to start with things I need you to do and why. If I start with kindness, I very well might not land the truth out of fear.

If I start with truth without interpretation and/or feeling, likely grace will follow, and then hope will lead to a constructive, productive conversation.

"You have a position here because you're important to our company. When I was your age and in a similar position, I made a ton of mistakes. I'd like to share with you what I learned. I'm here to help you do the best job you can, and I'd like to talk about how we can help each other grow."

Use this language with your employees, and you'll create an environment where, hopefully, annual reviews become obsolete. You won't need them. Giving immediate feedback inside of a situation—situational leadership—regardless of someone's position, is a gift, and let them provide it to you, too. Any employee should be able to walk up to the CEO of the company and say, "Hey, can I talk to you about something?"

Lay the groundwork for this type of culture, and you'll have an organization where people treat the receptionist the same way they treat the CEO.

WHY I HATE GLASSDOOR REVIEWS . . . AND ABSOLUTELY LOVE THEM

Feedback, on the other hand, always seems to have a negative connotation. That's why I'm not a huge fan of Glassdoor. Their anonymous employee reviews force you to focus way too much on the negative when you should be focused on the positive. That said, go ahead and read some of the reviews for your company to see if they bear any truth. But don't break down a disgruntled employee rant like a biology textbook. It's too easy for companies to get drunk on saying, "That's not true!" Read them, take what's useful, and then move on.

"I'm probably only going to be on this planet for about seventy-eight years," I told the assembled group. "I sure hope it's longer, but that's the average life span. That's it. After that, I'm gone. What's really important to me is to make sure I can drive by this building twenty years from now, walk in the front door, say hello, and feel like it's still the same place I left."

We were walking through a Glassdoor exercise together as a team.

As we began to read the comments, someone spoke up. "We *want* to become better leaders," one manager said. "We just need to know how."

I wanted to say, "Read a book. Get involved." But then they may leave thinking, *I have no idea which books to read. And how do I get involved? What does that even mean?*

"Well, we can start with Glassdoor," I said. "Are the statements in those reviews true? Are those points valid? If so, how are we going to bring our culture to light today and in the future? How are we going to build a sustainable path forward?"

Right when I finished, one of our developing leaders, Liz, walked in—six minutes late.

"Hey, I'm so sorry I'm late. Kids missed the bus."

I was right in the middle of talking about management improvement strategies. Then it hit me. I'm a fiftysomething male who's an empty nester. I'm telling everyone what I think we should do to grow our leadership skills. And here's Liz. Early thirties. Two small kids who dance and play soccer. She's got this big thing called life, and here's an old white guy giving her feedback on what to do.

"Hold on," I said. "Liz, you're frustrated because you were late?"

"Yeah, I'm really sorry."

"Well, you don't have to apologize to me. Because what I'd like to understand is what your options were for *not* being late?"

"Well . . . I didn't have any."

"I completely understand that! What a leap. What were you supposed to do? Not take your kids to school? Just leave them on the corner? Liz, you had no other options. The fact that you chose to serve your family over a job tells me that you have the emotional intelligence to make excellent decisions. We are a family-first place, right?" Life is a series of choices, and giving people a safe place to make good decisions is a noble quest. I told her, "Thank you for feeling safe to make good decisions. Thank you for believing in us, and thank you for sharing."

FEED IT FORWARD

Being prepared for the future is not the future's job; it is a job that is important today. The business and its people need clarity about who might be sitting in a leadership chair in the future. Often, you can be so close to the situation that you neglect to see what others see. Do others respect the future leader you might be tapping on the shoulder to the same degree you do? Does this person have the competence to lead, twist and turn, and think about the long game of the business, or are they too process oriented?

There are so many places to start. One that makes sense is poking around regarding how other people interact with them while you are around and, more importantly, while you are not, today and into the future. Feedback in the form of 360-degree reviews can be valuable and destructive at the same time. I am not sure using this process on the entire organization is important, but on a small set of future leaders, yes. The secret is to make sure you have resources and expertise to help you and others through the feedback and through the emotional roller coaster this process can bring.

Delegation of a big project is another way to experience potential areas for coaching. Spend some time to make sure of a few items, such as promising yourself you will not do the work for them.

Sometimes as parents, my wife and I got caught up with our children's projects and took over to make them look good, which, selfishly, was mostly rooted in making sure *we* looked good. Make sure people have the right tools, clarity, and direction. I don't always do a good job of explaining my vision for a project. Historically, I did not build check-in points, and when the project came to my desk, it wasn't even close to the canvas I had painted in my head. That is so unfair to me and others. Can you articulate with clarity a vision of your expectations, and are you willing to set those aside and let other people paint different colors on your canvas?

The power was not in the conversation between Liz and me, in my opinion. The power showed up when others watched us have an honest conversation about a situation. When someone is late, we, as leaders, often reflect back to our interpretation of being late. We pretend to know why they are late. *They are always late; here we go again.* We might think they are not taking this leadership thing seriously. Sometimes we're dead wrong, sometimes we are right—we will never know unless we ask the question. Having others see and hear this conversation was the real gift.

Like the janitorial services owner who bought company buses so her employees could get to work on time, it's important to stop and listen to your people. Too often, when problems arise, leaders jump into action with what they think is a great plan. But if we don't have all the information, if we're not the ones in the trenches every day, how good a plan could we hope to come up with?

Ask, don't tell. Hear, don't talk. You might be surprised at how much you learn.

JUST BECAUSE YOU HEAR DOESN'T MEAN YOU'RE LISTENING

As leaders, sometimes we forget about the lifestyle of our workforce. We forget the issues that our workforce faces. But we *can* understand them. We *can* get the feedforward (the reverse exercise of feedback) that we need. We have to ask the right questions and listen to the answers. No matter what industry you're in—listening is a skill you, your management, and your employees must master. But you can't expect someone to listen if they don't feel like *they* are being heard.

Instead of saying, "Here are some ideas on how to listen," ask, "How do you want your leadership to listen to you?" After all, what good is feedforward if no one's listening? Wouldn't it be great to ask your diverse workforce of younger audiences, older audiences, men, and women, "What can we do to become better listeners?"

I learned this lesson almost too late. As a Destructive Hero, I would give people feedback without telling them what they were supposed to be doing in the first place. That's how you become the mayor of Victim Hood. I'll tell you from experience, it's a terrible place to live. I got up every day and wrote a script for humanity like they were all actors in my movie. The problem was, nobody else knew I'd written lines for them, yet I held them accountable for saying them anyway. And when they failed to act the way I wanted them to, I resented them. It wasn't fair to them, and now I know it wasn't fair to me.

We need tools. A hammer is rarely a tool.

Today, through the grace of God and the help of so many people, I use tools to communicate. Those tools turn problems into opportunities. Not every problem is a nail, so not every solution can be a hammer. If you're going to communicate well with the people inside your organization, you need a variety of tools to solve a variety of problems. A few of my favorite tools are **empathy, fear** (yes, *fear*), and **rinse and repeat.**

LEAN INTO LISTENING

To start using **empathy** more effectively, put aside your own perspective. Try to see things from the other person's point of view. When we do this, we realize that other people aren't *try-ing* to be unkind, stubborn, or unreasonable—they're reacting to the situation with the knowledge they have.

Validate the other person's perspective. Once you see why others believe what they believe, acknowledge it. Remember—acknowledgment does not always equal agreement. We are beautiful and made to be different. Respecting those differences can lead to understanding. Understanding leads to growth. When we seek to understand versus seek to respond, we can learn so much about people and each other.

A recent example of this issue includes the controversy regarding the COVID-19 vaccine. Some people are apprehensive about getting the vaccine outside of a specific health reason or condition. Many of those issues I do not understand or agree with, but I am willing to acknowledge their truth versus my truth. We can accept that people have different opinions from our own and that they may have good reason to hold those opinions.

Then examine your attitude. Are you more concerned with getting your way, winning, or being right? Or is your priority to find a solution, build relationships, and accept others? Without an open mind and attitude, you won't find room for empathy.

A helpful acronym to remember how to empathize is **LEAN**:

- Listen with eyes, ears, face, and body (body language).
- Encourage others by being present, calm, and deliberate and by seeking to understand the other person's perspective.
- Attitude controls your ability to influence.
- Nurture relationships with your actions.

How can **fear** help make feedforward the new normal inside your organization? Fear is a tool. Our brains are wired to protect us, after all. Fear keeps Destructive Heroes thinking, *Me first!* in every interaction. As a result, no one feels heard. When leaders entertain fear, everyone loses. So instead of *listening* to fear, let's make our fear teach us how to make people feel *heard*.

Here is a helpful acronym to remember how to question **fear** and make that emotion your teacher:

- **Fight:** Am I willing to fight my fear in an authentic way?
- **Evaluate:** Why do I have these fears?
- **Act:** Can I take action against my fear with truth and optimism?
- **Rewire:** Can I learn from my fear and adapt?

Another valuable tool is **rinse and repeat**. To do this with your team, keep your question to one simple sentence. You can't talk about what *you* did this weekend until you (the listener) can repeat what the employee said. Most people can't do it on the first try. Usually, when you ask someone about their weekend, you wait for the other person to answer, and then you start talking about yourself. You see, your brain will choose what it wants to hear. Your brain will hear things you have done, and your mind will travel there whether you want it to or not. When that happens, you stop listening. And you miss so much.

Never be a story-trumper, interrogator, or selfish listener. When we are intentional about listening, we hear things under the surface, we see body language, and we see emotions. We step into that person's shoes and take every step with them. Try **rinse and repeat** at the office, try it with your spouse, try it with your friends, and try it with your children. Give them the gift of a better listener. God gave us two ears, one brain, and one mouth for a reason!

After our managers deploy listening strategies like this with their teams, those managers report back to us. They tell us what worked and what didn't. Your management may do a number of different exercises with their teams, and that freedom is wonderful. However, they should not all be based on the negative feedback your teams give you about management, whether on Glassdoor or in person. Now, as a leader, am I saying all middle managers are bad? No. Were the employees who posted on Glassdoor just wrong? I don't know. Regardless, we had middle managers we needed to coach and lift up. But instead of focusing on negative comments, we aimed to improve our group as a whole. After all, teamwork is the most effective leadership strategy on the planet.

360 DEGREES OF YOU

Our next phase of improving management was a 360-degree review for a few key leaders. If you ask your team about the management style inside your organization, you will hear (*if* you're a good listener) an overriding theme that needs to be addressed. Your optimistic believers will tell you, "This place is great. There are never any problems." But that's not entirely true. There are also people who bitch about everything. It's up to you to listen to everyone to get to the root of the issue. But sometimes, especially with a large workforce, you need a more structured place to start.

After we walked through this process with our leadership team, we sat down with our 360 results for a three-hour meeting. Now, these reviews are expensive. They take a lot of time. If you have a small company and you're worried you don't have the money or the time to do it, try to gain traction with the keep, stop, and start exercise explained earlier in this chapter. The 360-degree reviews might not even be necessary. But if your organization has many different departments where your culture can get muddied, they can definitely be worth the investment.

For our 360 reviews, our individual team leaders took a leadership test with the other members of their teams. Some of our leaders got high scores, and we said to them, "Hey, you're doing a really good job. What helps you overperform?"

But we also had leaders with lower scores. My scores were not perfect. Together, we discovered the source of the gaps. This was one of the best experiences I have ever been a part of, and it is still evolving. It is still evolving because perfection is a terrible destination. A 360 review can shed light on defects—areas we should work on and acknowledge. We can even get to a point where the gaps have been filled and we feel successful, but we are human, and chances are high, just like the game Whac-A-Mole, that other defects will show up. Acknowledge the process; it's a healthy one for a leader, a team, a mom, a dad, and a friend.

Despite any negative feedback, we never go to a whole team and say, "You guys suck." After all, the winners are sitting there thinking, *I'm not buying this. I'm working my tail off!* Remember those awful group projects in college? One or two students kicked back and slacked off while others worked hard to complete the project and get a good grade. The group score will tell you where the group's weaknesses are. You want your managers thinking, *How do we lift up our score as a group?*

During the 360 review, we all unzip our backpacks and dump them out on a desk. Big mistakes that everyone has made are all laid out in a series of meetings. Some people don't like that.

Help your managers understand *why* you're doing a 360-degree review and coach them through the results. Then give that team member time to improve their performance and then another 360 review. *How have I changed? Have things gotten better or worse?*

Some human resource professionals read employees' and managers' 360 reviews with them. I'm not a big fan of that because that relegates human resources to writing traffic tickets. No office needs that drama. Again, I recommend outside professionals who maintain strict confidentiality.

Keep conversations going about creating an environment where everyone is continually improving. Instead of telling someone, "Hey, I love what you did back in April," bring it up in April. Otherwise, that person stops listening and starts thinking, *Why didn't you have that conversation with me in April?* Feedforward is about keeping your communication open all the time. It's about listening to what your employees want and need to thrive in your organization.

If you decide to do 360-degree reviews, be careful. Keep everything anonymous. If anyone retaliates in response to criticism, make the consequences serious. This may sound like overkill, but anytime someone's blind spots are exposed on a single piece of paper, their emotions jump off a cliff. That's why you need professional counselors or coaches to read your team's 360 reviews to and with them the first time. That way, they can emphasize the strengths so the person doesn't tie themselves to a whipping post.

Fix the top 10 percent of your organization—management and up—and the improvements will flow like a waterfall down to the other 90 percent. If you give your managers the tools they need to lead their teams in a way that exemplifies your culture, then thirty years from now, when you walk through the front door, your company will feel like it did the day you left.

◆ ◆ ◆

Reflection: Let's Go Inside

1. "It's hard to give something away unless you own it in the first place."
2. Are you good at giving feedback? Why? How?
3. Do you store it up for a rainy day? Why? Why not?
4. Does feedback matter based on your role in the organization?
5. Is it easier to give feedback to people who are up or down? Why?
6. Is the feedback you give your coworkers different than the feedback you give your family?
7. Could you handle the feedback you give to others? Why? Why not?
8. Body language tells us so much. Lean into a conversation; try to listen like you had to repeat every word. Make eye contact, move your head to acknowledge what is said, and use your ears instead of your mouth to listen. Could you listen to repeat the conversation you hear?
9. Can you encourage others, including those who deserve it the least?
10. Can you check your attitude before leaning into a conversation?
11. How can you nurture relationships that are important to you?

CHAPTER 12

The Future-Proof Culture

Technology. Whether you love it, hate it, or both in the same day, there's no denying it's an integral part of all successful businesses. But even in an organization that appears to be 99 percent electronic, the culture, people, and user experience play unbelievably large roles.

Still, experts tell us that computers will replace 40 percent of all jobs by 2040. Most people read this and immediately fear job security for their children, grandchildren, and even themselves. But there's one thing they don't stop to consider—who's going to be building those computers? Programming them? Maintaining them? Fixing them? Let's face it: When it comes to technology, things will *always* go wrong at some point. When we touch technology, we expect it to work. Most of us have high expectations. Then we get frustrated when our tech doesn't live up to them. And then who do we call?

People. People manage technology to make sure it works. And those people don't work by themselves. They work with—you guessed it—other people! It takes human interaction to make sure computers and technology work. In fact, it's essential. If a customer has a problem or wants to speak to somebody, computers don't have the emotional intelligence to listen, respond, adapt, or inspire, no matter how good the voice-recognition software is!

EI, AI, AND HOW TO SAVE YOUR EMPLOYEES' JOBS

The emotional intelligence of your workforce has to rise along with technology. Customer support, technical support, and even marketing, shipping, and receiving. In any department, technology *will* replace the replaceable. There's no way around that. What do your employees do that's *not* replaceable? That *can't* be done by a machine? Answer these questions, build up these skills, and your company will rise, too. New technologies are coming whether we like them or not. Now, we could fight the trend, but that's not a good place to be. Instead of fighting or pushing, embrace them.

Think about any employee inside of your organization. Are they the type of person that people come to and ask questions? When a problem arises, do their coworkers ask for their help? Is that employee inspiring and encouraging? Optimistic and opportunistic? People like that will *always* have a job. As long as jobs exist, that employee can count on work. The position, department, and industry don't matter.

To make your employees so valuable they withstand competition from artificial intelligence (AI), automation, elimination, and outsourcing, increase their emotional intelligence (EI). Because for the time being, EI beats AI. For now, computers can't pull off human engagement the way *humans* can.

China is leading the world in facial-recognition and body language–interpretation software. I am not sure I have much confidence in how it is used today, but I believe this will evolve. Think about using technology for people development in a safe and effective way. More importantly, as we move into a deeper virtual world, we often have the tools to manage results, activities, and processes. This technology could begin to identify the emotion behind each of these. Emotions like truth, optimism, defeat, and aspiration. As those of us in North America introduce these technologies into our recruiting and hiring processes, those who fake it till they make it won't make it.

I love talking to students in college today. I ask them about what they are studying, their dreams, and their hopes for the future. I encourage them to look at classes that address emotional intelligence. In a world of bots and process improvement, emotional intelligence, in my opinion, cannot be automated. If it can't be automated and you have this asset, then that tells me you will have real value in your life and workplace. Only the emotionally intelligent—the authentic candidate—will win.

THE FUTURE IS INSIDE OF YOU

The first step to take in making your employees emotionally intelligent is becoming emotionally intelligent yourself. You can't tell someone to change what you are not willing to acknowledge inside of yourself. Remember the quote, "You can't act your way out of something you behaved your way into; you can only behave your way out"? Once again, don't be a hypocrite. Don't expect behaviors from your team that you don't exhibit yourself. To nurture a future-proof, emotionally intelligent workforce, embrace EI in your day-to-day tasks.

Manage yourself first.

Emotionally intelligent people begin with **self-management**. They hold themselves accountable to commitments. They possess self-control. They adapt well. Their positive outlook inspires those around them to self-manage better, too. No technology alone can do that.

The emotionally intelligent have **social awareness**. They

both empathize and sympathize. They feel others' pain *and* understand its source. They celebrate coworkers' successes. They do their best to solve problems and fix their mistakes. They fulfill their job responsibilities to the best of their abilities. Emotionally intelligent people know that even all-stars have a team, and they work together with their team rather than against it. *If the company wins, I win; if the company loses, I lose.*

Emotionally intelligent people master **relationship management**. They give and take. They handle conflict maturely—and privately. Even if they earn a meager salary, they mentor interns and inspire the C-suite alike. Identify your emotionally intelligent employees and treat them well. No algorithm can replace or displace them. But they *can* leave your company for a better position, especially if they feel like they're being taken for granted.

Finally, emotionally intelligent people possess **self-awareness**. The term *self-awareness* is so important because it is *not* the perception of others. It is the perception of ourselves and our ability to control our emotions. This includes our words, body language, tone, and so much more.

Emotionally intelligent people recognize their own emotions and observe how those emotions affect their performance on the job. More importantly, they open themselves up to feedforward and receive it well. It's critical to recognize how our emotions impact our ability to grow.

Managing our emotions is a learned response, not an inherited or instinctive one. Our past experiences can hijack us and get us into real trouble. Our brain reacts to situations at lightning speed, and the way we handle a situation is based on our past. However, our emotions do not react to *events*. Our emotions react to our *interpretation* of events.

For example, I love dogs. People at McGohan Brabender are encouraged and allowed to bring their pets to work. That's me . . . but what if I had been bitten by a dog when I was young? Chances are high that because of that event, I would have a different emotion.

Emotions are not neutral: they are either our master or our servant. The emotions we feed will be the ones that grow. The goal in emotional management is effectiveness, not emotional suppression or indulgence. Life without feelings or passion would be a dull wasteland of neutrality. What we need are the appropriate emotions—feelings that fit the circumstances.

People who heed their inner voice can draw on more resources, make better decisions, and connect with their authentic selves. **To be authentic is to be the same person to others as you are to yourself.** In part, it means paying attention to what others think of you, particularly people whose opinions you admire and who will be candid with their feedback. But some of us care way too much about what others think of us, and we trade masks, depending on the person to whom we are speaking. This is a relationship based on others' opinions and lacks a relationship with ourselves, which is the most important relationship we will ever have.

What does that mean? It means great leaders have an open awareness. They know what is going on around them and don't get caught up in one particular thing. They don't judge, censor, or tune out—they reflect.

Understanding our own inner resources and limits helps us grow into a better, different tomorrow. Honesty with yourself about what really happened and your part in it—that's the secret to greater emotional intelligence.

Really. I used that word above for a reason. You see, our emotions (if not understood and reflected upon) will tell us fake stories. We've all experienced it. But if we don't get control of this, we limit our ability to seek the truth.

◆ ◆ ◆

THE MIRROR IS A WONDERFUL
PLACE TO FIND A FRIEND

Reflection is the lens of truth. What if we could take a situation and watch it before it happened? Do you think you would change anything? You bet—and that is the gift of reflection.

First, it's power. Reflection is the catalyst that jumpstarts self-directed, personalized (i.e., meaningful) leadership. Adding reflection to the mix increases your chances of experiencing the aha moment you're hoping for.

Sounds good, but how do you induce reflection? It's not as easy as creating a reading list, teaching a class, or facilitating an exercise. You can't force someone to reflect in a meaningful way. You can, however, set the conditions for meaningful reflection to occur.

Whether you're in charge of developing other leaders or are developing yourself, this truth still stands: education and experience are important, but if you aren't injecting your life with adequate doses of reflection, it will never become self-sustaining, let alone create positive results.

Reflection allows us to grab life and learn from it. Mistakes will happen. We all make them. Always have, always will. The gift of those mistakes is passing those lessons on to others. To lead other people, you first have to get good at leading yourself. And the key to leading yourself is to engage in periodic self-reflection. Unless you pause from time to time to look at how you're doing, you won't know what you need to be doing differently in the future to be better.

Use your reflection not as a torture chamber but as a useful tool. Acknowledge mistakes and work through them; don't ignore them. This process allows us to look back on our mistakes so they can be useful to ourselves and others. It's a beautiful tool if you have the courage to move forward.

Self-reflection is often the difference between being

busy and being productive. Often, we fill our lives with activities to feel like we are busy, but are we effective? Or put another way, self-reflection transforms activity into productivity. (Go back and read it again!) It enhances your leadership because you become more aware of the decisions you're making as a leader, and that, in turn, generates greater transparency. You can make great decisions rather than being forced into quick ones that could end up being viewed as shortsighted and inferior.

How will engaging in self-reflection help you as a leader?

Self-reflection can serve as a wake-up call for you. As parents, we do this all the time. Based on our experience, we want the very best for our children. What if we had the same mindset for ourselves? Self-reflection can simply be a reference point we look at every day. Ask yourself: Where am I, where was I, and where can I be better tomorrow?

It can remind you to live your life more fully in the present rather than obsessing over things you can't control that may (or may not) happen in the future. That process of reconnecting will make you a better leader because you'll be more aligned with what's happening all around you.

I find it helpful to get what's in my head onto a piece of paper. Thoughts lose a lot of power when they're voiced with people you trust or written down. When the crap hits the fan, journaling is the best way to reflect and understand what happened, why it happened, and how you could have acted differently. Think of a journal as a toolbox. A way of truthfully remembering events and how they made you feel—and what actions you took.

I have a journal. I often go back and look at past years. Honestly, I read what I wrote and feel grateful I am not that person today. Now, some people don't like journaling. I get it. If that's you, don't worry about keeping a consistent journal. When a conflict arises, just write down what happened, how you felt, what your part was, what you would have done differently, and what tools you have for next time. No need to do this in a formal journal if it's not your thing.

NOT JUST A TOOL, BUT A WAY OF LIFE . . .

After Abraham Lincoln died, his colleagues found a box of Lincoln's "hot letters." He wrote down his emotions about people on paper and put them aside until he cooled down. Most of the letters Lincoln wrote, he did not send. Most great leaders have written letters like these and have *not* sent them.

In today's world, we have a technology we should be very careful with: *email.* It would be hard for a letter to go viral, but emails, on the other hand, *can* and *do.*

We're going to talk about two different strategies to help you and your team increase your EI. To avoid sending an email you might regret later, I recommend an exercise called the **learning circle** by LifeShape designed by Mike Breen and 3DM Ministries. I use the learning circle every day. It keeps me centered on my side of the street. Recall that your brain is like a bad neighborhood—you shouldn't be there alone. This learning circle is your friend—but *only* if you're willing to be honest with yourself.

Use the learning circle to unpack emotions of fear, sadness, anger, hurt, and pride in the privacy of your own thoughts or journal. These six pointed questions can help anyone figure out which side of the circle they're on—and where they should go next.

1. **Observe:** What happened?
2. **Reflect:** How did it make me feel, and what was my part?

3. **Discuss:** Whom can I talk to? Whom can I trust to hear truth, not cause drama?
4. **Plan:** How do I clean up this mess or learn from it and move on?
5. **Accountability:** Who will hold me accountable for what I said I would do?
6. **Action:** What will I do?

Most of us stay on the right side of the circle. That means you only have a conversation with yourself, which often can be dangerous. The right side is admitting you're wrong or you have been wronged. Stay there, and Victim Hood is your home. This is a terrible zip code to live in. If you want to move, honestly look at where in your life you are selfish, self-seeking, dishonest, and the *big* one—*afraid.* Just like the good book says, the truth will set you free.

Move to the left side of the circle. That's where real beauty and acceptance show up. You must be willing to talk about what happened, acknowledge your part in it, and ask for advice from someone you trust (your truth teller) about what to do next. As I said earlier, I have Beth Ferrin, our CFO and, more importantly, a dear friend.

You can choose to take the advice or not, but moving forward without advice (or time to understand yourself and others) keeps you trapped. The learning circle allows you to move forward. It's not our job to fix the world; it's our job to fix ourselves.

LIFE HAS TERMS; LEARN HOW TO EMBRACE THEM

Life is interesting, and we have to deal with it on life's terms. Sometimes life's terms get us into a spot where normal function is difficult, like when Liz showed up late to that meeting. Often, when someone else doesn't appear interested in interacting with us, we can say it's our fault. It's normally not. When we seek to understand each other instead of making snap judgments, beautiful things can happen.

Not sure who at your company fits the EI bill? Let me give you a couple of examples.

Skill x effort = results

Employees with high EI multiply their efforts and skills to produce results. They treat their jobs like an equation. They know trying hard isn't good enough. When they improve their skill set, they're essentially growing their worth. You, the employer, rents that skill set, but you don't *own* it. If the rent goes up, it's up to you to scramble to keep that asset.

An emotionally intelligent workforce acts as leaders, not followers. At McGohan Brabender, we expect employees to step up and take action, not sit back and shrug, thinking, *Not in my job description, not my problem.* Leadership is an inside job, which means it starts at the top—you.

Leaders are busy and often juggle many responsibilities at a time. That can be a talent or a curse. Sometimes we're so busy that our life looks messy and disorganized. We think, *One day I'll clean it up and life will be simpler*—but that day doesn't come.

I love power washing. I adore the instant gratification. You get to look at something dirty and neglected and watch it start to look like new. When you're finished, it's very satisfying. Your life can be the same way. This might not be as fast as a power washing, but it will be just as satisfying. It didn't take minutes or days to clutter your life, your work, or your people. It took a long time. If you want to be an emotionally intelligent leader, give yourself time. I promise you'll be glad you did.

The same is true with other parts of your life: your car,

your garage, your closet. Clean them up one step at a time, one project at a time. Get organized physically, and you'll be organized mentally, too.

EI is understanding you, your role, and your influence on others. Remember the Four Cs of your culture heroes—character, chemistry, competence, and collaboration. The Four Cs also instill strong EI in your entire workforce.

We want our workforce to manage the emotions that drive their behavior. **Emotionally intelligent people manage their emotions so their emotions don't manage them.** They don't lose their emotions; they use their emotions. The secret is *you* have to want it more than they want it. People will always do more of what they see versus what they hear.

Easier said than done, right? Everyone says things they wish they could take back. I have too many stories to tell you about the lessons I have learned. Like emails, I wish there was a button to undo the statements we have written or said. I get into the most trouble when I project my assumption of what the other person is feeling or thinking onto them. Imagining what an employee is thinking can carry us into dangerous waters.

To help your team manage their emotions, give them permission to get quiet anytime—right in the middle of a meeting, an argument, or anywhere. Getting quiet slows us down and allows us to think even when words are being thrown at us from the other side. When you do speak, start from the beginning. It is amazing what happens when you stay on target and try to address the real issue.

Positive feelings + positive energy = positive action

Disruptive feelings + negative energy = negative reaction

You choose to learn to grow your EI. It's a journey, not a destination. When our attitude is right, there is no barrier too high, no challenge too great, and no circumstance too difficult to prevent us from achieving our best self.

TELL STORIES TO TECHNOLOGY-
PROOF YOUR WORKFORCE

Today, when people are overwhelmed with state-of-the-art technologies and mounds of data, they are moved more by a simple story. The best way to connect with and influence anyone is to tell them an engaging story that appeals to their emotions.

An appealing story is a purposeful story with a mission in mind. And most importantly, it must be a story you believe. If you don't believe it, you're manipulating people!

Create an amazing vision, and if you want to add a little tabasco to the mix, tell a great story. People buy stories. They remember stories. Write your story and tell a compelling one. I took McGohan Brabender's values, vision, mission, and brand and told a story that is compelling, not just interesting. The passage below is the script for a video where we tell that story.

> We Are MB
>
> WE ARE . . . a huge small place. A whoever-you-are-you're-welcome-here sort of place. A sense-of-family place, a friendly place. A home-away-from-home, maybe-a-second-home sort of place.
>
> WE ARE . . . a beyond-words place. A we-can't-be-pinned-down-to-one-thing place, where knowledge is king, communication is respected, and teamwork is coveted. An inexpressible place. A place where people are encouraged to grow in real and unexpected ways.
>
> WE ARE . . . a befitting place, where generations mix and swirl, where spirits strengthen, minds stretch and sharpen. A place where friends are made, children are welcome, and you can pet a friendly dog if you like.

WE ARE . . . in three cities, shaping and shifting to meet the need. We're not rough and tough. We're simply asked to do four things really well: provoke people to think differently; reveal new opportunities; encourage action that expands social responsibility; and provide a clear path that people can see, hear, and, more importantly, feel.

WE ARE . . . called to provoke the comfortable and comfort the provoked with our minds, ears, voice, and touch. We are defining simplicity in a complex world. We are bestowed trust to have character in everything we do, to serve people when they're ready, to smash a complex world into one beautiful, connected story, and to take a risk to expand our responsibility for each other and the people we serve.

WE ARE . . . serving 100,000 employees, 250,000 "belly buttons," and 1,200 employers. You will find us empowering business with solutions to propel the economy. Empowering people with choices to create healthier workplaces and communities. Our aspirational gift to all, including each other, is to deliver healthier birthdays to people, organizations, and communities.

WE ARE . . . the spirit and the mind of good, smart people effectively managing the entire healthcare dollar. A place where change is inevitable, progress is honored, and life just gets better for all.

Trust me on this. WE ARE MB!

Have the courage to write a story that sticks with customers. This isn't just a McGohan Brabender thing. Volvo is one of the largest car companies in the world. Do you know how they sell to their consumers? They don't run flashy sales ads. They keep it simple. A Volvo is the safest vehicle that gets you from point A to point B. Every product manufacturer tries so hard to sell to us. But it's those who tell a story that stick in our minds. What do you think about when you think about a Volvo? *Safety.* They tell that same story over and over again. When given the choice, people will choose to buy compelling stories every time.

If you can learn to prepare and deliver purposeful stories well, then you'll have no problem moving people. You don't need state-of-the-art technologies to connect. It's the state-of-the-*heart* technology that's the game-changer.

In the rising trend of a technological takeover, the world still needs quality human interaction to offer the best customer service (and employee experience) possible. Will your employees embrace EI? If they do, will you work hard to keep them? Nurture your organization's culture, and you'll be doing just that without even thinking about it.

You can't fight change. And if you don't like change, you're going to like irrelevance even less. But you *can* build the right car for an amazing ride.

Reflection: Let's Go Inside

1. If you could rate your emotional intelligence level today on a scale from one to five, what would your score be?
2. Where is your weakness?
3. Where are your strengths?

4. How do you get garbage out of your head today?
5. Could you try the learning circle? Take a situation you are dealing with in your head and walk around the circle.
6. Observe—What do you see? What do you feel?
7. Reflect—If you could go back in time, would you change something?
8. Discuss—If you had to bring this conversation up with someone, who would that person be?
9. Would that person hold you accountable to change?
10. What action do you see yourself taking?
11. What is the best story you have created in your life?
12. What is the best story you have created inside of your organization?
13. Is there a story that others missed?
14. Is there a story by someone else in your organization that you could help tell others?
15. What is the story you want to create for YOUR life?

CONCLUSION

The Mirror Is a Wonderful Place to Find a Friend

I lived much of my life as a chameleon. I did not love myself, so everywhere I went, I changed colors to fit in. I built masks to wear in every area of my life. To me, it seemed normal, and I thought I had tricked everyone. I had a mask for work, home, the golf course, church, and the list goes on. I was wearing myself out and slowly destroying everything that was important to me.

I didn't have the capacity or the energy to attempt to address my issues mask by mask, role by role. If I wanted to be a strong leader, husband, father, grandfather, brother, and friend, I had to surrender it all.

Loving yourself isn't arrogant. It's a gift. Take it from a guy who hated himself so much he nearly gave up. Years ago, I sat on the floor of my bedroom closet, sobbing and believing no options besides quitting existed. It was terrible. By far the worst day of my life. I begged God to take away my pain. I was tired, lonely, and afraid.

Suddenly, I felt something wash over me. I didn't see a light or hear a voice, but I had this overwhelming *sense* that I would be OK. Now, don't get me wrong. I didn't get up and forget everything I was feeling. I felt *different*. I felt like I had an option. I knew this would suck, and the path to find myself would take brutal honesty, hard work, and vulnerability. Most of all, it would take time. It took me forty-two years to screw myself up; it would take time to repair a past and build a future. But it was an option I was willing to take.

In that moment, I wanted to remember everything I felt. I ripped part of my shirt sleeve off and placed it on the shelf in my closet. That sleeve still sits there today as a reminder of the darkest place I've ever been. I know now that by pushing away selfish thoughts and loving myself and others through life's journey, I'll never have to go there again. And for that, I'm so grateful. The journey *was* hard, but today, I know that I'm OK.

Sometimes, I hear similar stories from people who've been in that dark place. The hard work we accomplish every day is a reminder of the life God wants us to live here on earth. My relationships with my wife, my children, our workforce, my friends, and myself have changed since that day, and for the better.

It was worth it. Today, I always show up at meetings when I say I will. I always call people back when I say I will. And I treat Victoria and every other employee the way they want to be treated. I know because I've asked—and they've told me the truth, thank goodness. Most importantly, I am not perfect. I am a human being with character defects and a desire to grow myself and others, and I am very capable of making mistakes.

The Bible says, "A fool shows their ignorance at once." Not in a day, a week, or a month—at once! I was a fool. *True ignorance is not the absence of knowledge, but the perception that you have it when you do not.*

The information I had was self-taught and made-up—lies

I told myself about me, others, and the world. Understanding yourself and God is a foolproof way to face the world and be useful to it.

When it's all said and done and you leave this world, you won't get to take anything with you. I'm pretty confident of that. I'm not saying material things don't matter. But memories matter more—the ones you make and the ones you leave behind. My memories only go back two generations. That doesn't mean my grandparents' parents—three generations ago—didn't make a dent in this world. I'm sure they did. I never met them. The simple fact is, we're not here that long. Creating a legacy shouldn't be born of ego or pride. Only a legacy of character, friendship, kindness, compassion, and love will last.

I know now what a meaningful legacy is. But for the longest time, I went about it all wrong. If you are like I was, you wear a number of masks—a mask for work, a mask for home, a mask for the golf course, a mask for friends. But none of these masks is the real you. Some of these masks get heavy. One might feel more comfortable than another, so you wear that one most often. That's when life gets complicated—for you and for the people around you.

When you surrender these masks, it's one of the few times in life you get to give up and *still win*! That surrender takes real courage and a boatload of truth. Is it easy? No. Is it worth it? Every single second.

Leaving a meaningful legacy is more than handing people money or owning cool possessions. Your legacy is a journey, not a destination. And that journey begins with truth. Masks are not the real you. If people didn't buy into the last mask you wore, there is little chance they'll buy into a new one. Surrender those masks. You don't need them!

We, as leaders of organizations, have even more work cut out for us—our legacy includes the living, breathing culture we leave behind. For many of us, the journey of building a culture begins with a desire for compliments from others. What are those words of affirmation you want to hear from others? Write them down and look at the difference between today's reality and tomorrow's goal.

Don't tell the world this difference—work toward your goal in an authentic way. The difference between who you are today and who you need to be tomorrow is your culture gap. In this gap are your blind spots. Find truth tellers close to you whom you trust to see and feel what you can't. Trust them, but also trust tomorrow's self. Often the greatest company cultures on our planet started with the power of one! They transform the naysayers, bystanders, and victims into believers. You *are* allowed to change yourself right now. You don't have to be the same person tomorrow that you were today.

Start with your family. There's nothing worse for your family than seeing you treat everyone around you better than you treat them. If you don't have this curse, be grateful—because many leaders do.

Think about ways to help people understand your new mission, vision, and passion for your workforce. Think about the five senses of culture. People should be able to see your culture, taste it, hear it, and feel it. People can already smell your culture—especially if it stinks!

Words on the walls are terrific, but only if they're honest. Birthday cards, handwritten notes, and even a "Happy Birthday" sung by the CEO will brighten every spirit in the office.

Instead of avoiding tough issues, run toward them—hard economic times, industry disruptions, even deaths in the family. Remember, when you're afraid, *move*. Move toward the issue, not away from it.

Tell your workforce over and over the dream culture you

want to achieve together. When you're tired of saying it, you might be halfway there. Keep going! Is it authentic? It should be! Will it be perfect? I hope not!

Build a culture with a cause. It's best to find a cause that's both close to your heart and close to your mission as a business. Make it matter to the world around you. Remember, your cause is *never* about profitability. I've seen so many organizations hit hard times, and their cause is the first thing to come off the truck. A real cause, nurtured with passion and heart, should *never* be eliminated.

Find a team of culture heroes, and turn around at least one naysayer, bystander, or victim. When you reform just one of them, you create an environment where other turnarounds follow.

Document your culture's stories and tell them over and over again. People love stories. People want to be part of them. Allow your people to be in the next chapter of your culture.

When you create a work environment that's attractive to everyone inside, you can sell that environment to anyone on the outside. Your ability to attract great talent for your workforce can be part of your culture! Sell it like you sell your product.

Feedforward is much better than feedback. Many companies have feedback processes after the fact that sound a lot like a judge and jury. *Feedforward* is an honest, humble, authentic word of affirmation to make us better and stronger.

Your culture is your legacy. Anyone can create a wonderful culture. You don't have to be the owner or the head of HR. I promise you, if *you* want a wonderful, creative, enthusiastic culture that builds and binds a workforce, you can start building it all by yourself. If you're authentic and loving, I can't imagine anyone stopping you.

If business is about people—products are created and innovated by people, manufactured by people, shipped by people, processed by people, bought and sold by people, and thrown away by people—shouldn't your culture be about people? It's as simple as that.

A culture that magnifies your heart is your quest. It could be your legacy. So do your best. That's all anyone can expect of you. Go create something amazing, something that makes a noise where Boom Bands are playing, as Dr. Seuss would say. It's worth it because your company is worth it, your people are worth it, and so are you!

BONUS

Culture Through the Lens of a Crisis

On March 10, 2020, I was driving my car home from a trip with my wife, Lori. The news was speaking about COVID-19. As of that date, there were no deaths in the US, but the global impact was moving across the ocean and Americans were asking big questions with little or no answers at our fingertips.

While we live in a world of questions, most often, we can swiftly find the answers we want to hear. In March, any answers seemed rife with agendas.

I didn't know where to go for answers, and the news could slant my opinion one way or another. Asking others wasn't much different. Who had the truth or a fair analysis for a next step moving forward?

I say this because our organization created a culture, a culture of time, trust, faith, confidence, courage, grace, and care for people, our customers, and our communities. The culture of our organization was asking us a question. The question was simply, "How will you react to this information?"

I am not a huge fan of politics, and by the grace of God, I have tools to help me make decisions without being tilted by the color red or blue. Let's just say a confident lens of purple is what I look for.

I called two people I trust: Jon Husted, the lieutenant governor for the great state of Ohio, and my dear friend, the mayor of Dayton, Nan Whaley. My question wasn't deep and profound, just simple and to the point. "As a leader, what should I do next to protect our workforce and our community?"

The answer was just as simple as the question. "Scott, this is a real threat to all of us, so if you could stand behind the decisions we make together we would be grateful."

AN ORGANIZATION HAS A HEARTBEAT

Once upon a time, there was a person . . . well, maybe not a person like you and I would imagine. For the time being, let's call it an organization. I say this because I am not sure you can see its face or hear its voice, but maybe you can. The culture of an organization is the sum of its actions, its behaviors, and its character during good times and what rears its head during the roughest of times.

The organization doesn't learn these traits on its own; they are not innate like a mother raising a child. It does not have a diploma and has little authority over anything or anyone.

The organization does require a degree of formalization. For example, to operate effectively, it must file with many forms of the government: the federal government, the IRS, the state it operates in, and local regulations.

It protects itself and its owners from liability and is held accountable for its actions. It carries a name, a reputation, and an identity that is separate from its parts or its people.

Everyone has touched one or been a part of one at some

time or another. It can carry confidence, trust, fear, anxiety, fun, excitement, or just plain dullness.

Where did the word *organization* come from?

Etymology is the study of the origin of words and how they have evolved. The *Online Etymology Dictionary* says that the term emerged in the English language in the mid-fifteenth century. At that time, it meant "act of organizing." The word came from Middle French *organisaton*, which came directly from Medieval Latin *organizationem*. In 1873, it assumed the meaning "system, establishment."

The word originally came from the Greek *organon*, which means "organ."

The definition is simply:

"A company, business, club, etc., that is formed for a particular purpose."

Organizational theory is all about a relationship between organizations and their people. The most important is the power of people, and at the highest level, the organization is held accountable for its purpose, actions, opinions, and impact on people, places, or things.

Why is this important? *What Smells in Here?* was written prior to COVID-19. COVID-19 doesn't make culture any more important today than it was before; however, the lens of a crisis defines a culture.

As organizations, the media, and individuals were coming to their own decisions, we waited on the next steps forward.

On March 16, we were told the state of Ohio was likely ready to call an order to stay at home. At McGohan Brabender, we could have waited for an order, but great cultures shouldn't wait for an order to move. They move based on the inherent traits of their past, present, and future; they move with heart.

After spending over two hours debating the decision to work remotely, understanding we would be defined as an essential employer and with only a fraction of our workforce currently working from home, we decided to order the work-force home.

The communication path was even simpler. We outlined what we needed and expected, and we decided to build a timeline to make this work for ourselves, our people, and our customers. That timeline went to the side immediately as we simply pulled a video camera into our office, read from our notes, and asked our workforce to:

- Go home and be safe
- Stay up to date with the CDC, WHO, and state guidelines
- Take care of our customers
- Forward all calls to their cell phones
- Be responsive to all people
- Stay in contact with our strategy as it evolves

Within thirty minutes, that video was sent to our work-force via email, and within the next hour, the entire workforce was safe at home.

The last several years, McGohan Brabender has had a strategy to move from desktops to laptops. We had watched our workforce use this technology with customers more often, and it seemed like the right move. I would like to say we were smart, but honestly, let's just chalk this up to being more lucky than smart.

Our access points depended on the workforce having VPN access, phones that could be transferred, and video conferenc-ing that could be transferred to employees and our customers. We didn't know the answers to many of these questions before we sent people home. We were just hopeful that good, smart people could figure this out.

Within hours, additional VPN access codes were pur-chased, mobile hot spots were secured in case people had problems with home internet access, and video strategies such as Zoom and Microsoft Teams were lifted up and expanded.

We assembled a MB Response Team of people who would meet daily to address the issues as we understood them and update our course of action moving forward.

That evening, we asked our senior IT systems administrator to keep track of the access points from our workforce every three to four hours. We trust our workforce because they trust us, but if we didn't have a handle on how people were working remotely, trying to maintain a structure over time would be even more difficult.

During our MB Response Team call first thing on March 17, IT told us 90 percent of our workforce had signed on and were working prior to the call. Now I have had a lot of amazing things happen over my career at McGohan Brabender, but that number took my breath away and brought tears to my eyes. We didn't have a remote strategy for the entire workforce and didn't have time to figure it out before we sent people home. We had to trust ourselves that sending people home was the right thing to do and our people would stand tall and do their best.

FOCUS MATTERS

They did their best before, and their best was evident in the midst of not having many answers or a solid solution.

Our response team met daily on video calls. Every day was a different challenge, and the questions just got bigger as we evolved together.

The number one question was: Could we maintain our workforce as it was today? We didn't know the answer to this question, and we were smart enough to know our workforce had this question even if they didn't specially ask. If there is one thing I have learned about leadership, it is simply: "Do not leave people alone in their thoughts."

Our first step was to review our customers one by one and make an estimate at the potential layoffs, reduction in force, furloughs, and/or top-line revenue reductions. This was easier than we thought, so we went deeper into each account by industry and by location. Our methodology continued into what this might look like over a ninety-day period, 180-day period, and the overall impact over twelve months.

What was interesting about this process was the fact that the state of Ohio had not ordered people to stay at home, and no one had an idea regarding how long a stay-at-home order would last. Looking back, the diligence to expose our truth about the economic situation gave us a sense of confidence that would allow us to maneuver with our workforce intact.

It also meant there were expenditures that we should address to keep a workforce over other initiatives we had in store.

An article written in 2008 by the *Harvard Business Review*, "Roaring Out of the Recession," spoke directly to the recession and the success of organizations that fought through it: who won, who lost, and who survived. What was interesting is the organizations that immediately reduced headcount were the *least* successful in returning to a thriving business. The *most* successful had a strong balance between reality and growth.

We communicated directly to our workforce about our best attempt to keep everyone at MB with us through the crisis. We addressed it fairly and swiftly, and the communication was right on target, including answering questions we knew they were thinking. Why not simply call them out honestly and timely?

Additionally, our response team was asked to call every employee directly every week with a rotating schedule. It meant each of us had nineteen phone calls per week. It did not sound like a lot at first, but it took more time than we thought.

However, the gift of those phones calls is a gift none of us will ever forget.

We were like a lot of other organizations that walked through this process. We deployed objectives to be responsive to our customers and be respectful of a workforce that was trying to teach children online and take care of customers at the same time.

We built a strong strategy to the best of our ability and continued to move forward day by day. Day by day turned into week by week, month by month.

Coffee chats were important so we could see each other. Our culture was created by people, built by people, and we needed people to grow and nurture our culture. Scheduling events to not only listen to each other but to see each other was valuable.

Our annual awards ceremony, named the eMB'ys (a creative name for MB to celebrate), means so much to us. We celebrate the accomplishments of our business and, more importantly, our people. This event is normally live and has over 175 people in attendance. We dress up in evening gowns and tuxes. In 2020, it was once again an amazing event, even though the entire ceremony was held on Zoom and the dress code was shifted to pajamas.

Like many organizations, we tried to be intentional about our strategy to connect. We talked to other companies, borrowed their ideas, watched social media for creative solutions, and were in constant contact with our staff to make sure our strategy was not too much, not too little, but just right.

LIVING THE MB CULTURE

Although as leaders, we were harnessed with decisions we had never made before, our staff taught us the most.

They raised over 180 days of notes, questions, and issues, and the questions they asked *us* and the questions we couldn't answer made us feel less alone. We weren't alone in this process; so many organizations just like MB were in the same situation. I would say we were not the smartest or the most prepared, but we began to see the value of our culture through a different lens.

Our values were established in 2003, and we have been proud of them for decades. In the midst of chaos, we thought it might be an interesting process to ask our staff to explain our culture to us. We asked them to choose one word and to use that word in a sentence.

We were amazed at the responses and the details they put into the effort. I remember sitting at home on a Friday night. I can't stand having emails unread on my phone. I am not sure if it's a curse or a blessing, but having more than ten gives me a small panic attack.

As I glanced at the phone—quite frankly, wanting to delete a few to get my number to less than ten—I noticed seventy-eight unread emails in just over an hour. I wasn't sure how much detail would be included and if the comments would mold into anything meaningful. I was wrong; I was dead wrong.

I began to read their emails and, honestly, began to cry. You know the type of crying that comes from joy, pride, and a sense of belonging. One by one, I read them and began to feel like the values we defined in 2003 had to include this contemporary language.

As I said before, MB's original values were set in 2003. They were defined, communicated, and articulated inside the walls of MB. It was the foundation of what we believed to be true about our people, our customers, our vision, mission, and brand.

The MB leadership team believed it would be important to

reestablish our desire to remain independent. We had an opinion as a group, and those opinions were thought to be wide and different. It was critical to reset these opinions into clear, concise thoughts as a group, and establish an MB Ownership Covenant. This work was compelling and concise, and everyone was in alignment to carry MB into the future boldly as an independent, privately held organization.

The MB covenant was established to ensure the shareholders had a strong desire to remain independent. The next important step was agreement on how we would behave culturally, together. We decided to do the hard work of defining what Living the MB Culture means to the business, our people, and us as shareholders. We assembled a Living the MB Culture team that went way beyond a group of shareholders. This group included a diverse segment of our business by gender, age, position, and personality balance or PI.

We were armed with a purpose statement and four equal objectives.

> Living the MB Culture Purpose Statement
> The MB Culture is what has carried us forward for almost five decades. We our passionate about remaining fiercely independent. In order to protect our independence, we will boldly anchor the MB culture utilizing the vision and the stories of our people including: MB's geography, MB's demographics, MB's business segments, MB's current values, MB's Vision, Mission, Brand—for today and for our future, together.

> Our Target
> A strong, vibrant, courageous, and timeless

culture should instill and animate four leading principles.

The MB Culture enables us to achieve our desire to remain fiercely independent.

The MB Culture supports us in achieving our Vision, Mission, Brand and critical strategies.

The MB Culture allows our workforce to adapt to change.

The MB Culture empowers a workforce to thrive and perform.

This group went out into the workforce to ask questions and collect stories, and as a group, we began to understand the power of making this come alive even more.

The language that was returned to us was more contemporary, progressive, and quite frankly, more exciting than the words we use today:

Family

Integrity

Knowledge

Teamwork

Communication

We collected this language and grouped the words into four categories:

Family

Trust

Innovation

Service

We carried this as far as we could, but there was a sense the words weren't powerful, contemporary, and meaningful enough. We needed deeper tools with clear explanations to help our people lead each other. We were so close, but it lacked the language to make what we care about sing and make noise, as Dr. Seuss would say, "to the land of Boom Bands."

We pushed and pulled, worked on the language and the descriptors, and most importantly, made sure we could utilize these values in three ways:

- Recruiting language that inspired people to want to be a part of our organization
- Culture language that was descriptive to all of us regarding how we interact with each other—and tools to help those who don't, work themselves in or out
- Customer language that inspired people to do business with MB and explained what our values, our core truths, mean for them

This is important work, not because it's fun, sappy, or what I enjoy doing. It is important because it is the foundation of any organization. Processes, strategies, budgets, governance, and measurable increments are valuable in a business. However, only people can exceed your wildest dreams, and only people can make you feel great at the end of the day. Everything we value in life and in business begins and ends with people.

These are the beautiful words we heard about **Family**:

- Caring fun
- Playful
- Compassionate
- Community
- Honest
- Team close-knit
- Commitment caring for the whole person
- Respectful family-oriented decision-making

- Correct priorities
- Celebrating others' accomplishments
- Willingness to share the load and help the team
- Treating employees like an extension of our family
- Taking care of employees before, during, and after challenges

These are the words that **Trust** solidified:

- Accountable transparent
- Candid honest
- Dependable
- Reliable
- Flexible earned
- Resolute confidence
- Assurance
- Respectful
- Can't be bought, trust is built over time
- Freedom to make a choice
- Gained by asking for, listening to, and acting on feedback
- Trust is a shared responsibility between all team members
- Confidence in each other to do their jobs well
- A pattern of clear communication and positive decision-making

What does **Innovation** mean to our people?

- Curious
- Brave
- Courageous
- Agile

- Fearless
- Insightful
- Visionary
- Positive
- Future-focused pacesetter
- Bright resilient
- Incremental changes over time make a big difference
- Anticipation, being ahead of the game
- A spirit of positivity is a necessity
- Proactive instead of reactive
- A team that's prepared to answer questions before they're asked

Why **Service** is so important:

- Responsive
- Empathic
- Intentional
- Urgent
- Purpose-filled taking initiative
- Servant leadership
- Valued
- Knowledgeable
- Flexible
- Customer-centric
- Effort
- An attitude that is Main Street, not Wall Street
- Anyone can learn how to care
- Smiles can be heard even through a phone call
- Customers know when you care about them and when you don't
- We exist to outperform and outserve
- Your attitude dictates your actions

All of this language tugged at our hearts and minds and led us to a new way of thinking. That new way of thinking brought to life a new set of values. A set of values we will call **Our Core Truths**:

Using Uncommon Sense
   We mutually empower each other by trusting our jobs to be done.
   We communicate clearly with honesty and transparency.
   We foster a community of listening and accountability.
   We build trust over time—earning it through actions.

Making the Future Brilliant
   We believe our industry belongs to the curious and the brave.
   We optimistically imagine the future and work to bring it about.
   We accelerate innovation through preparation and collaboration.
   We are fearless—overcoming failure and setbacks with grit and determination.

Cultivating a Culture of Care
   We serve with empathy, flexibility, heart, and hustle.
   We advocate for our customers because we're on the same team.
   We believe exceeding expectations is the least we can do.

We gauge our success through improved lives.

What makes these words even more beautiful and brings them to life is the fact that leadership did not design or pay for them. These are the words from our people, from their hearts. We simply arranged them.

The impact of COVID-19 will continue to provide learning experiences for us as an organization, and I am confident it will serve as an anchor in so many ways.

A NEW, EXCITING CHAPTER FOR MB

While writing this chapter, I am finishing up the final communication to announce a remote work strategy for the entire organization. We were on our way with a remote strategy, but there is no question COVID-19 accelerated this process.

Culturally, this situation requires all organizations to manage and adapt. We are not alone in this boat. Simple issues such as attire at home versus work, making sure people know the value of keeping their laptop and computer cameras on inside of the building and out, and the preferred timing for non-business-related activities.

The list will go on. I am not a big fan of rules, but there are places where clarity is more important than brevity.

Lastly, today is May 9, 2021. COVID-19 woke up those who were ready to listen, watch, learn, and feel. Most businesses had a hard time remaining in business or even harder remaining independent. A recent study indicated the life span of a business today, independent of COVID-19, is eighteen years.

Just like your organization you feel is special, we feel ours is, too, and we would like to protect our business to assure it moves off into the future.

We explored many options to protect us. As shareholders of McGohan Brabender, we set in concrete a shareholder covenant. Basically, a promise to our families, our workforce, and each other to remain independent.

This evolution led to a restating of our values, which are now called our Core Truths. Finally, we hired a consulting firm to conduct a study to help us understand how other organizations make it past the eighteen-year mark.

They interviewed our workforce to make sure they wanted McGohan Brabender to move off into the future. We felt its importance, but did they? They did. The responses were beautiful, heartwarming, and compelling. Most importantly, they had little to do with what we did and more to do with how we treated, loved, and cared for each other along the way.

We explored how accounting firms, law firms, manufacturing firms, and consulting firms like McGohan Brabender perpetuate. Over the past ten years, over seven thousand organizations just like McGohan Brabender have sold to Wall Street or private equity. That's not our style or our desire, and if we were called to give back to a community that gives to us, it is hard to do that from the East Coast to the West Coast.

Our options were immense, but the direction was clear and even more compelling. The target began to swing toward an ESOP—an Employee-Owned Organization. Our workforce always acted like owners, and for the most part, owners always acted like employees. We thought and verified everyone behaved this way, and everyone had a similar mindset. We believe in moving an organization beyond those of us who are here today. How could we drive pilings deep into the ground to assure the waves of the future wouldn't or couldn't change our course?

As I sit here on May 9, I cannot wait to announce the most exciting news in the history of our organization. On June 15, 2021, we will bring our entire workforce together and walk through a history of our organization. A beautiful story of where we came from, where we are, and where we are going.

On that day, we will announce our newest owner, our entire workforce. As a fifty-six-year-old, thirty-two-year employee of McGohan Brabender, I cannot think of a better, stronger message to protect what we have built together. To assure jobs will stay in each community we serve. To provide investments back to our customers and not Wall Street or private equity. To provide a barrier that a compelling financial metric to sell will be rinsed through an entire workforce and not simply those with the biggest chips on the table. Lastly, to continue to create beautiful stories for ourselves, our customers, and our communities that go way beyond those of us who are here today.

I can understand the impact of COVID-19 on our world, our country, and our communities. Many organizations were dispersed and still haven't recovered, and some may not ever be restored. Factually, I understand the loss of life and the families that were impacted, and the memories this terrible virus stole from so many. I think of the financial consequences of our youth, and the toll this will take on future generations. The list could go on, and I do not want anyone to think COVID-19 gave me or our organization a gift, because it did not.

If COVID-19 handed us anything, it was an opportunity to refocus, realign, make brave decisions, and walk through the dark together. We saw people in their homes, dogs, cats, kids, doorbells, and all. If there is one phrase I have come to despise, it is simply, "You're on mute." If I never hear that phrase again, I will be a better person.

Thank you to the people inside of McGohan Brabender who trusted us to move through this together. I know we made mistakes, but if I had to go back, I believe we got the big decisions right. If my son or daughter worked for an organization like McGohan Brabender, I would be grateful for them for three reasons. They would be surrounded by good, smart people who care, they would be protected from the organization selling to an outside organization, and they would have a place where they know themselves and their families are welcome.

Reflection: Let's Go Inside

1. Looking back, what did you learn about yourself during COVID-19? What are you most proud of? What are you not proud of?
2. Did you watch others make poor decisions, and what impact did they have on you or others?
3. What were some of the best decisions you witnessed or were a part of?
4. If you could go back knowing everything you know today, what would you change?
5. Looking forward, what will stay important to you in your life and as we evolve?
6. "All great changes are preceded by chaos." What changes will you make?

ACKNOWLEDGMENTS

Thank you to my wife, who gave me a chance and loved me when I was probably hard to love. Thank you to my children, who showed me grace, and to my entire family, who encouraged me.

Thank you to Mike Mathile, who, while having a cup of coffee one morning, encouraged me to write a book. Mike, it was a challenge, and I am grateful you pushed me.

Thank you to the shareholders and the people of McGohan Brabender; you trusted me and gave me confidence. The culture of this company is a combination of the culture that was handed to us and everyone's desire to move it forward. I wish I could list everyone's contribution because I have so many wonderful stories. Trust me when I say I could not be the person I am today without you, and McGohan Brabender wouldn't be the organization it is today without your hearts and passion.

APPENDIX: SAMPLE EMPLOYEE SURVEY

1. How long have you worked for MB?
   a. Less than one year
   b. One to four years
   c. Five to nine years
   d. Ten to fourteen years
   e. More than fifteen years

2. What position do you currently hold at MB?
   a. Service representative
   b. Account manager/ARM
   c. FAS team member
   d. MB advocates member
   e. Accounting, commissions, and payroll/compliance/marketing
   f. Administration/EHL/front desk/facilities and operations/HR and training/IT
   g. Sales/BD
   h. Prefer not to specify

3. I have a good understanding of the company's vision.
   a. Agree
   b. Partially agree
   c. Partially disagree
   d. Disagree

4. How confident are you in MB's future?
   a. Extremely confident
   b. Confident

    c. Not confident

    d. Extremely unconfident

5. My manager gives me constructive feedback on my job performance.

    a. Often

    b. Sometimes

    c. Rarely

    d. Never

6. My manager gives me recognition and praise when I've done a good job.

    a. Often

    b. Sometimes

    c. Rarely

    d. Never

7. How often are you fully utilized in your current role?

    a. All of the time

    b. Most of the time

    c. Some of the time

    d. Rarely to never

8. I am encouraged to take action when I see a problem or opportunity.

    a. All of the time

    b. Most of the time

    c. Some of the time

    d. Rarely to never

9. The MB Organization Chart has increased my understanding of the internal structure of the company and the relationships among individuals within MB.

    a. Agree

b. Partially agree
c. Disagree
d. I have not seen it

10. I truly enjoy my team! We are productive together, communicate well, and have fun.
    a. Agree
    b. Partially agree
    c. Partially disagree
    d. Disagree

11. How likely are you to recommend MB as a place to work?
    a. I have already
    b. I am thinking about it
    c. I am unlikely to
    d. I never would

12. How would you rate the benefits that are offered to MB employees? Please rate each of the following, with 5 being "Excellent" and 1 being "Very poor." (Please mark N/A if you have not utilized or do not receive the specified benefit.)

    • Medical __
    • Dental __
    • Vision __
    • 401(k) __
    • Other (short-term and long-term disability, LegalShield, EAP) __

    Please specify why you rated an item 3 or below:

13. The training, education, and development opportunities that I've received this year from MB have increased my capacity to be successful at my job and have helped me grow as a professional.
   a. Agree
   b. Partially agree
   c. Partially disagree
   d. Disagree

If you indicated "partially disagree" or "disagree," please provide additional information:

14. I feel the performance review process gives me constructive feedback and guides me to be a better employee.
   a. Agree
   b. Partially agree
   c. Partially disagree
   d. Disagree

15. I feel the three companywide bonuses motivate MB employees to help further grow the business by increasing sales, retaining business, and doing so profitably.
   a. Agree
   b. Partially agree
   c. Partially disagree
   d. Disagree

16. I feel I am compensated appropriately for the work I do at MB.
   a. Agree
   b. Partially agree

c. Partially disagree

d. Disagree

17. How would you rate the communication and transparency within MB (e.g., HRD updates, employee meetings, segment meetings, team meetings, town hall meetings, unpacked videos)?

a. Excellent

b. Good

c. Poor

d. Very poor

18. What can MB do better? Please include recommendations for how we can execute these changes.

NOTES

1. Denise Lee Yohn, "2018 Will Be the Year of Employee Experience," Forbes, January 17, 2018, https://www.forbes.com/sites/deniselyohn/2018/01/02/2018-will-be-the-year-of-employee-experience/#4fcaf411c8fc.
2. Jena McGregor, "Only 13 Percent of People Worldwide Actually Like Going to Work," The Washington Post. October 10, 2013, https://www.washingtonpost.com/news/on-leadership/wp/2013/10/10/only-13-percent-of-people-worldwide-actually-like-going-to-work/?noredirect=on&utm_term=.8493993efb6d.
3. Pew Research Center, "Labor Force Composition by Generation," May 11, 2015, https://www.pewresearch.org/fact-tank/2018/04/11/millennials-largest-generation-us-labor-force/ft_15-05-04_genlaborforcecompositionstacked-2/.
4. West Midland Family Center, "Generational Differences Chart," http://www.wmfc.org/uploads/Generational DifferencesChart.pdf, accessed September 29, 2021.
5. West Midland Family Center, "Generational Differences Chart."
6. West Midland Family Center, "Generational Differences Chart."
7. West Midland Family Center, "Generational Differences Chart."

ABOUT THE AUTHOR

Scott McGohan, CEO and cochairman of McGohan Brabender, melds his decades of experience in leadership and business into his mission of improving the workplace for all.

Also active in community outreach and service, McGohan was honored with the 2022 People of Vision Award by Prevent Blindness. He is both the founder of and a mentor with the Mentors Matter summer camp, which serves inner-city youth in Dayton, Ohio. A former board member of Crayons to Classrooms and Coastal Pet, McGohan is a current board member for the YMCA and Dayton Development Coalition.

A former TEDx speaker, McGohan writes and speaks on company culture, sharing his skills in vision casting, strategy alignment, and leadership deployment.

Made in the USA
Middletown, DE
05 September 2023